"Stephan Bodian draws t subject: the peaceful and liberating ground of awareness in which experiences come and go. His own great depth of insight and heart comes through on every page as he offers clear descriptions of subtle matters, practical suggestions, and experiential practices. Truly, a jewel of a book."

—**Rick Hanson, PhD**, author of *Buddha's Brain* and *Hardwiring Happiness*

"This provocative and profound book shines a light on how practicing meditation can reify the doer—the self who is being mindful. With great lucidity and care, author Stephan Bodian introduces approaches drawn from non-dual wisdom traditions that allow us to relax back and realize the indivisible radiant awareness that is already and always here."

—**Tara Brach, PhD**, author of *Radical Acceptance* and *True Refuge*

"Stephan Bodian takes us beyond mere words, ideas, and mental fabrications into the very heart of the matter. I heartily recommend this excellent book."

—**Lama Surya Das**, best-selling author of *Awakening the Buddha Within* and *Awakening to the Sacred*

BEYOND

MINDFULNESS

THE
DIRECT APPROACH
TO LASTING PEACE,
HAPPINESS, AND
LOVE

STEPHAN BODIAN

NON-DUALITY PRESS
An Imprint of New Harbinger Publications

Library of Congress Cataloging-in-Publication Data

19   18   17

10   9   8   7   6   5   4   3   2   1   First Printing

Dedicated with boundless gratitude to my teachers,
without whose patience and generosity
this book would never have come to be,
and to the peace and happiness
of all beings everywhere.

Contents

Foreword

It may be hard to imagine what lies beyond mindfulness practices and teachings, especially given how clearly beneficial and pervasive they are. Isn't it enough to bring open, nonjudgmental, and curious attention to our present experience and to cultivate loving-kindness? Certainly for some it is. Yet others, whether long-time practitioners or beginners, may sense that there is a more direct path to freedom, love, and happiness. If you are such a reader, you have found a superb book and a worthy guide.

Stephan Bodian, a dear friend and colleague whom I met on retreat in the late 1980s, thoroughly walked the path of mindfulness as a Zen practitioner and priest. He went on to study with non-dual spiritual masters from the traditions of Tibetan Buddhism and Advaita Vedanta, including our mutual teacher Jean Klein, as well as to become a licensed psychotherapist. As a result of this rich and varied background, he offers what may be the first of its kind—an insider's critique of mindfulness meditation and teachings that is both appreciative and challenging. More importantly, he eloquently points to an inherent wakeful awareness that underlies the practice of mindfulness—the jewel teaching of this book.

There is much to appreciate about mindfulness teachings and practices. For many, these have been their first introduction to meditation and the dharma—a portal to their inner depths and to a deeper truth. Mindfulness develops a more spacious relationship to thoughts and feelings, reduces anxiety and depression, and improves concentration and open-heartedness. In some cases, it has led people to realize their true nature. However, it can easily leave us in a mode of striving to improve ourselves. After all, we can always be more mindful, can't we? This tendency to want to "better" ourselves presents a huge potential pitfall. We can easily remain in a subtle state of lack rather than recognizing our inherent wholeness.

It turns out that the essential qualities that mindfulness practitioners try to purposely cultivate, such as wisdom and compassion, are spontaneous byproducts of awakening to our true nature. Deep self-inquiry is like the process of uncovering a pure spring. Upon careful investigation, the distinction between self and other softens and dissolves. As a result, clarity, love, and a profoundly wakeful and luminous awareness naturally emerge. At first we may feel like we are no one—undefined and unconfined—an infinitely open and free space. In time we also discover that we are not separate from anything or anyone. This realization is far beyond seeing that we are interconnected on a phenomenal level—that is, that we are part of a greater whole. Rather, it is the intuition that the seer and the seen, the knower and the known, are not two. We experience ourselves as the pure light of awareness, the source and substance of all phenomena. This is the fruition of heart wisdom. Of course it takes time for this understanding to transpose to the conditioned body-mind.

As we awaken from the trance of the separate self, we naturally welcome what is—life as it appears—and find ways to creatively respond that break the cycle of reactivity. This shift affects both our residual psychological conditioning and our responses to events and people in our daily life. Where before we may have approached our troublesome thoughts and feelings as something to change or get rid of (another form of reaction), they are instead honestly faced and innocently welcomed, just as they are, into the light of awareness. What happens when you feel deeply seen and accepted? Our rejected parts and patterns respond in the same way.

As we discover our inner freedom, we naturally offer it to others. So, too, with our self-acceptance and love. Happiness and peace effortlessly radiate out as a spontaneous, unselfconscious blessing.

Enjoy the illuminating words in *Beyond Mindfulness,* and the Silence from which they come. With Stephan's skillful guidance, may you recognize and more fully embody your true nature.

—John J. Prendergast, Ph.D.,
    author of *In Touch: How to Tune In to the Inner Guidance of Your Body and Trust Yourself*

Introduction

For many years I practiced mindfulness meditation as a Buddhist monk. For hours each day I paid careful attention to the coming and going of my breath and to the sensations of my body as I meditated. I became adept at noticing thoughts and feelings as they occurred and found myself feeling calmer, more spacious, and more disengaged from the drama that had seemed to be my life. In time my customary anxiety diminished, and a sense of ease and contentment enveloped me. My relationships improved, my mind settled down, and my concentration deepened. Instead of worrying about the future or obsessing about the past, I lived increasingly in the moment, focused on doing the next task as carefully and mindfully as possible. From a nervous intellectual, I transformed into a paragon of patience, groundedness, and equanimity. I was a completely different person.

At a certain point, however, after years of mindfully following my breath, studying the subtleties of meditation with some excellent teachers, and teaching mindfulness myself, I reached what I felt were the limits of mindfulness. I had certainly become calmer and less reactive, but I also found myself feeling more disengaged from life, as if I were experiencing it at a distance, rather than being immersed in the immediacy of the moment. My meditations were definitely more focused and free of mind chatter, but they seemed somehow dry and lacking in aliveness and energy. When I described my experience to my Zen teacher, he merely told me to meditate more. After considerable soul-searching, I decided to set aside my Buddhist robes and meditation cushion and study Western psychology. I knew there were other ways of working with the mind and heart, and I wanted to learn what they had to offer.

Several years later, after dabbling in other forms of Buddhist meditation, I was introduced by a friend to a teacher of nondual wisdom from outside the Buddhist tradition who advised me to stop practicing mindfulness and directly inquire into the nature of reality. I was intrigued by his words, and by the deep silence I experienced in his presence, and I set about following his guidance. One day, while I was driving on the freeway, a phrase he had often repeated, "the seeker is the sought," drifted through my awareness. Suddenly my reality turned inside out. Instead of being identified with the little me inside my head, I realized that I was the limitless, unconditional, ever-awake awareness in which the thoughts and feelings I had mistakenly taken myself to be were arising and passing away. Even though I was no longer meditating, I had stumbled upon the experience I had been seeking for so many years through meditation. Had my years of practice informed this moment of fruition? I have no doubt. But meditation alone turned out to be insufficient to reveal the secret I was struggling to unveil.

This book echoes my own journey of seeking and finding, and it draws on my many years of guiding others in discovering what cannot really be taught, only evoked and realized. Although I found mindfulness extremely helpful for living in the present moment and easing my turbulent mind and heart, I ultimately had to go beyond it to discover the peace, love, and happiness I was seeking. The title is meant to be provocative but in no way to diminish the exceptional benefits that mindfulness confers. For beginners to meditation, I still recommend cultivating a mindfulness meditation practice as the most effective way to work with stress, anxiety, depression, grief, anger, and other challenging emotions and mind-states, gain insight into the causes of suffering, and achieve relative peace and equanimity. But for a variety of reasons that I discuss at length in this book, lasting fulfillment may elude you unless you go beyond mindfulness and come to rest in what I call awakened awareness.

Many of the best-known teachers of mindfulness in the West appreciate this perspective. Influenced by nondual teachers and teachings from the Buddhist and other traditions, they caution against practicing mindfulness *instrumentally*—that is, simply as a method to achieve some more desirable future state.

Instead, they point to a noninstrumental perspective where mindfulness opens you to a dimension of inner wisdom you already possess but merely need to access. Some even use the term "mindfulness" as a synonym for awareness itself. They teach that the practice of mindfulness ultimately takes you beyond mindfulness in the conventional sense to the realization of awakened awareness. For the most part, however, these teachers don't offer a critique of mindfulness. And they don't provide the more direct approach that I describe in this book.

HOW TO USE THIS BOOK

I've structured this book to mirror the retreats I lead: Each chapter features teachings, guided meditations, and dialogue. The teachings use words to point beyond words to our natural state of awakened awareness. The meditations, which are interspersed throughout the chapter, invite you to step beyond your conditioned mind to experience a direct glimpse of awakened awareness for yourself. And the question-and-answer sections, which are set apart at the end of each chapter, address topics that need further elaboration. If you want to get the maximum benefit from your time in these pages, I suggest that you resist your habitual tendency to accumulate new beliefs and concepts and instead let the words bypass your conceptual mind as you allow genuine insight to blossom. Immerse yourself in the teachings, stop from time to time to practice the meditations, and turn to the dialogues to get answers to some of the questions that come up as you read. May the truth described in these pages come alive for you, and may the book guide you on the direct path home to the peace and happiness of awakened awareness.

A NOTE ABOUT MINDFULNESS

For the purposes of this book, I've chosen to critique the progressive form of mindfulness that's widely practiced these days in secular settings and many retreat centers worldwide, and then to contrast it with the direct approach described in these pages. But for some teachers, the deliberate practice of mindfulness is a natural stepping stone to a more spontaneous, effortless, and self-sustaining level of awareness that's essentially identical with what I present in this book. Ultimately, mindfulness itself, when practiced under the guidance of a teacher who knows the direct path home, can take you beyond mindfulness to your natural state of awakened awareness.

CHAPTER 1

The Limits of Mindfulness

*Once you recognize the bright sun of awakened awareness,
practicing mindfulness can seem like shining a flashlight at
midday in the hopes that it will make things brighter.*

In the context in which I learned and practiced it, mindfulness
was always a stepping stone, not an end in itself: a skillful method
for going beyond mindfulness to recognize the foundation out of
which mindfulness arises. According to this tradition—which
can take a number of different forms but in my case expressed
itself through Zen Buddhism—the act of being mindful is a portal
to a deeper, enduring awareness that can't be manufactured or
practiced. This deeper awareness is always functioning, whether
we know it or not. Indeed, it is our natural state of spontaneous
presence, without which there would be no experience at all.
Instead of cultivating it like a talent or strengthening it like a
muscle, we just need to recognize and return to it.

In this context, mindfulness is not designed to maximize performance, improve health, boost mood, or confer any of the other
benefits scientific studies in the past several decades have identified. Even relative happiness and other positive emotions, an inevitable result of regular mindfulness practice that the traditional
teachings acknowledge and value, are themselves considered a
means to a more ultimate, fulfilling end: the recognition of our
true nature and the "sure heart's release" from suffering. The other
benefits are just side effects, perks on the path to self-realization.

Mindful attention to the arising and passing away of experience can yield penetrating insight into the impermanent, insubstantial nature of the so-called material world and of the collection
of thoughts, feelings, memories, and images we take to be a separate
self. In some approaches to mindfulness, this insight is generally
achieved only after years of concentrated meditation practice. But
there's a more immediate approach that points directly to this
deeper level and invites an instantaneous recognition, beyond the
mind. This more direct approach to lasting happiness and peace of
mind is the province of this book. Mindfulness may prepare the
way, but at a certain point you need to go beyond mindfulness.

MINDFULNESS IN THE WEST

As it's currently practiced in the West, mindfulness derives primarily from the Theravada Buddhist tradition of Southeast Asia.
Originally the Pali term *sati* (generally translated as "mindfulness") included the sense of remembering (to be present) and also
of discriminating between desirable and undesirable mental and
emotional states, a connotation it still holds in many traditions.
Mindfulness as "bare, nonjudgmental attention to present-
moment experience"—which is how it's taught in Vipassana
retreats, Mindfulness-Based Stress Reduction (MBSR) courses,
and most secular mindfulness trainings these days—emerged as
the principal approach in the West through the influence of
several Buddhist masters and the Western teachers in their
lineage, who brought it from Asia in the mid 1970s. At about the
same time, Vietnamese Zen Buddhist monk and Nobel Peace
Prize nominee Thich Nhat Hanh began teaching a similar
approach to mindfulness in Europe and the United States.

Although these approaches differ slightly, they share an
emphasis on practicing and cultivating certain mind-states in

order to become wiser and more compassionate—and, in secular versions, to reduce stress, improve health, relieve depression, maximize performance, and achieve the other benefits of mindfulness practice.

The direct teachings presented in this book take a different approach: You already are the love, compassion, wholeness, health, and happiness you seek—you don't have to practice to become it; you just need to recognize and be it. Easier said than done, of course, and I devote the chapters that follow to guiding you on this direct journey home to where you've always been. But the direct approach is significantly different from the progressive path generally taught in the mindfulness tradition and has a very different effect.

The difference between the direct and progressive approaches can be summed up in how they understand awareness. For the mindfulness traditions, awareness is generally viewed as a means to an end, a faculty you learn to cultivate to achieve a calmer, more compassionate, more focused state of mind—and ultimately to develop insight into the impermanent, insubstantial nature of reality. For the direct approach, which can be taught in conjunction with or as a follow-up to mindfulness, awareness is not only a function or faculty, it's the end of all seeking because it's what you are, and what reality is, fundamentally. When awareness awakens to itself through you as the essential nature of Being itself, you have reached the fruition of your search and come to abide as awakened awareness. The faculty of mindfulness as a remembering of what you are may continue to operate, not as a practice you do, but as a spontaneous homecoming.

Just be who you always already are—that's the mandate of the direct approach. The practice of mindfulness is not a prerequisite. All you need is a healthy curiosity and a dedication to discovering the truth for yourself.

THE BENEFITS OF MINDFULNESS

These days mindfulness is being marketed as an effective remedy for the stress and malaise that plague us as denizens of the digital age. And for good reason: Numerous studies demonstrate that the regular practice of mindfulness can enrich our lives in countless ways. Aside from the more obvious subjective ones like enhanced enjoyment of life, more harmonious relationships, reduced stress and anxiety, and relief from depression, research demonstrates that it actually changes the brain in significant positive ways. Simply by paying nonjudgmental attention to your experience on a regular basis, you can completely turn your life around for the better.

Perhaps the most significant and far-reaching effect of mindfulness practice, one that can't be measured by EEGs and fMRIs, is the growing tendency to see your thoughts and feelings for what they are and no longer take them quite so seriously or personally. Ordinarily, we're completely seduced and enthralled by our thoughts and feelings and mistake them for reality; with mindfulness, you learn to develop a certain healthy space or distance from them. This slight space allows you to be present for the ideas, images, fantasies, memories, and emotions that skitter through your awareness before responding to them, rather than immediately getting hijacked by them and allowing them to control you.

For example, a friend or family member says something brusque and inconsiderate, and your immediate reaction may be to feel shocked, hurt, shamed, or incensed. Instead of pausing to be aware of your feelings and the thoughts that accompany them, you may lash out in anger and get into an argument that lasts into the night. Or perhaps you withdraw, distance yourself from the other person, and sulk, as your mind fills with negative judgments and criticisms. With mindfulness, you may be able to catch the feelings as they arise without reacting to them, and then reflect on them calmly before responding in a more appropriate way. Instead of being lost in your feelings, you learn how to develop a healthy relationship with them. Dubbed *emotional intelligence* by psychologist Daniel Goleman, this ability to relate to your feelings in a spacious, balanced way and communicate them clearly without reactivity is a skill highly prized in boardrooms, workplaces, and families around the world.

In addition to its value in the cultivation of emotional intelligence, the spacious awareness cultivated in mindfulness practice has inestimable value in other practical ways: It helps chronic pain sufferers gain distance from their pain; enables innovators and creative thinkers to shift outside the box of habitual thinking; and allows people who suffer from stress to gain perspective on challenging situations and thoughts and explore more fruitful ways of responding. But even mindfulness has its limits.

MEDITATION: Being aware of awareness

Awareness is at the heart of both mindfulness and the direct approach. In this meditation, you have an opportunity to shine the light of awareness back upon itself, notice how awareness functions, and reflect on who or what is aware.

Find a quiet, comfortable place to sit for ten minutes or so. Take a few deep breaths, and allow your attention to shift from thoughts and feelings to the sensations of the coming and going of your breath. If your mind wanders off into thought, gently bring it back to the breath.

Notice how your attention keeps wandering off and returning. Be aware of the movement of attention as it shifts from one thing to another, from thoughts to feelings to sensations and back again. In other words, be aware of awareness itself. In doing this, you're accessing a level of awareness that's prior to your usual habitual awareness.

Now ask yourself: If I'm the one who's aware of my thoughts, who is it who's aware of the movement of awareness? In being aware of the thinking, am I not completely outside of the thinking process itself? Can I locate the one who is aware? Just sit with this inquiry and see what arises.

THE LIMITS OF MINDFULNESS

In the beginning, mindfully shifting your attention again and again from thoughts and feelings to the sensations of the breath helps you counteract an old habit with a new one. Accustomed to fixating on the stories, fantasies, daydreams, and memories that play out in your head, you're now focusing instead on sensate experience, which is more immediate and more directly connected to the present moment. Over time this attentional shift brings you into a more harmonious relationship with your body and your bodily felt experience and entrains you to pay attention to what's happening right now, rather than to your interpretation of what's happening.

Unlike thinking, direct sensation is a portal to the present, whereas thought generally transports you to an imaginary past or future. As your practice matures, you're able to expand your awareness from sensations, both inside and outside your body, to include thoughts and feelings as well, without getting caught up in them. This is the spacious awareness discussed earlier.

At a certain point, however, the practice of mindfulness, as a particular state of mind that you need to keep making an effort to maintain, can begin to seem laborious and mechanical, and you may find yourself longing for a more spontaneous, less manipulative way of being present. When I was a monk, I became so focused on maintaining deliberate attention to my present-moment experience that I lost my natural ease of being and morphed into a kind of mindful automaton. Not until I let go of mindfulness did I discover a more relaxed, effortless quality of presence. No matter how beneficial, techniques can only take you so far, and the goal of mindfulness is not better and more concentrated mindfulness, but greater openness, spontaneity, and authenticity. Buddha likened technique to a raft designed to take you to another shore. Once you arrive, you don't need to carry the raft around on your head but can leave it behind on the bank.

When properly taught and practiced, mindfulness can be soft, gentle, spacious, and compassionate, as I described earlier, and a good teacher will guide you in gradually relaxing your effort, at least to some degree. Only our achievement-oriented conditioning tends to turn the practice into something obsessive. The habit of focusing on a future goal and regarding meditation not as an opportunity to be still, present, and open to the moment, but rather as a task-oriented methodology for achieving some distant end, runs deep and dies hard. This goal orientation defeats the very purpose of mindfulness, which is to invite you to be present for your experience without judgment, interpretation, or agenda. The growing buzz about mindfulness's benefits and the impressive research results run the risk of turning mindfulness into another self-improvement scheme, another task on your endless list of things to do, rather than an opportunity to shift from doing and accomplishing to just being.

At a subtler level, the emphasis on the deliberate application of attention, while helpful at first, has a number of potential pitfalls and limitations. For one thing, it may gradually reinforce a new identity as a detached observer. Rather than breaking down the apparent barriers that separate you from others and the world around you, mindfulness may actually reinforce them by giving you the sense of being a separate observing ego, localized in the head, looking down mindfully on your experience and actions from above. Instead of inviting you to be more intimate with life and other people, mindfulness can become a kind of deliberate, habitual distancing that robs you of warmth and spontaneity. As one Zen master puts it, "If you are mindful, you are already creating a separation. When you walk, just walk. Let the walking walk. Let the talking talk. Let the eating eat, the sitting sit, the working work."

This pitfall is a subtle one that even the most experienced meditators (indeed, especially the most experienced meditators) have difficulty recognizing. The key word here is "ego": Spacious awareness without fixation somehow morphs into a fixed position (ego) that perpetuates separateness. People who fall prey to this fixation may become identified with their detachment and be difficult to reach, even in intimate relationships, where they tend to withdraw from genuine, spontaneous interaction. During my years as a monk, I felt proud of my status as a longtime meditator and hid behind the detachment I had cultivated to avoid being vulnerable. The difference between spacious awareness and detached observation is crucial here, but it can be tricky to discern: Spacious awareness relaxes the sense of separation and fosters greater warmth and intimacy with what is; detached observing creates distance, aloofness, and a subtle (or not so subtle) aversion to what is.

Related to this fixation on detachment is the tendency to use mindfulness to avoid or actively suppress emotions that you find uncomfortable or threatening. Rather than facing and welcoming them, as mindfulness is actually intended to encourage, you develop a level of concentrated awareness that enables you to rise above and seemingly transcend them entirely, whereas in fact they continue to roil beneath the surface and ultimately get expressed in unconscious ways. Perhaps you've met meditators like this: the coworker who bubbles with grief and pain she's kept at bay but claims her mindfulness has put her above such petty human foibles; or the close friend who claims he has no anger but periodically erupts in rage and then quickly returns to an enforced quiescence as if nothing has happened. When I finally realized that meditation wasn't helping me to deal with certain difficult emotions, I left the monastic life to study psychology and explore other options. The ability to manipulate attention, which mindfulness teaches, can become a tool to control your inner life and may lead to *spiritual bypassing*—the use of meditative methodologies to bypass more everyday, human concerns.

As a Buddhist monk, I met many people like myself who resorted to meditation as a refuge from life's challenges, retreating to their meditation seat when the going got rough to follow their breath and calm their turbulent mind and heart. Unfortunately, they never took the next step and used the penetrating insight that meditation provides to investigate the root causes of their discomfort and angst. Indeed, some people become addicted to meditation—admittedly, as addictions go, not a bad one to have—and believe they can't function without their daily fix of mindfulness. As soon as they have an emotion or mind-state they find uncomfortable or undesirable, they feel they need to fix it by meditating it away.

If you practice mindfulness meditation regularly for months and years, you may fall into the habit of engaging in a kind of mindful autopilot, a routinized watching that robs awareness of its natural unconditioned openness and spontaneity. Employed in this way, mindfulness just perpetuates your dependence on an altered state that needs to be constantly maintained, and it never really empowers you to experience abiding peace, freedom, and authenticity, which are after all the ultimate promise of mindfulness.

When used as directed, of course, the regular practice of mindfulness can be extraordinarily helpful in seeing through the filter of thoughts, feelings, and stories that separate you from others. But these pitfalls—the tendency to identify with being the separate, aloof, mindful watcher; the tendency to turn meditation into a goal-oriented task; the tendency to suppress challenging thoughts and feelings to maintain an enforced tranquility; and the tendency to fall into a kind of habitual, conditioned attention —may become deeply ingrained and difficult to recognize or shake. The term "mind-ful" itself can fuel these misconceptions by seemingly localizing the process in the head. You may be able to sustain your calm, detached observing through constant vigilance, but when your energy flags and you relax your effort, the observing state and the calm it perpetuates begin to flag as well— until you once again make an effort to be mindful.

TRANSITIONING TO THE DIRECT APPROACH

Many people are quite content with engaging in mindfulness meditation on a regular basis and see no need to pursue it further by attending retreats or otherwise extending or deepening their practice. Others may attend an occasional retreat and become adept at sustaining spacious awareness but continue to feel quite comfortable within the usual mindfulness framework. Still others may feel drawn to pursue mindfulness in one of its incarnations as a path of insight into the nature of reality.

If you're reading this book, however, you may be one of those who have reached the upper limits of mindfulness. Perhaps you feel stuck in one of the pitfalls, but no matter how hard you try, you can't break free using the mindful techniques at your disposal. Indeed, you may feel like a dog chasing its own tail, using mindfulness to free you from the pitfalls of mindfulness but never catching up. One of my students described it like this:

> I'd been meditating for years, and I was able to stay mindfully present for hours on my meditation cushion. In everyday life I felt lucid and calm but somehow detached; I couldn't really feel my own aliveness or the warmth of connection with others. I felt like I'd hit a dead end, and I didn't know how to proceed. My teacher just told me to continue meditating, but I knew this wasn't what I needed.

Or maybe you're appreciative of the spacious awareness you've discovered but weary of the constant doing, the addiction to maintaining a certain state, and you wonder if there's a way through or beyond mindfulness to a deeper, more natural, and more self-sustaining level of awareness. Or you may experience moments when your mindfulness spontaneously drops away, you lose touch with the observer entirely, and you effortlessly find yourself beyond spacious awareness in a kind of no man's land without a reference point. These moments can feel disorienting and unsettling, and you may end up grasping for your mindfulness again.

MEDITATION: Resting in the gap

Generally the mind is filled with an uninterrupted flow of thoughts and feelings that can feel overwhelming or oppressive. If you practice mindfulness, you may gradually develop an inner spaciousness that allows you to breathe deeply and negotiate the flow. In the direct approach, you may spontaneously discover natural spaces or pauses between the thoughts where an inner silence and stillness reveal themselves effortlessly.

Take a few minutes to sit quietly and pay mindful attention to your breathing. Now turn your awareness to the cascade of thoughts and feelings. Even though it may feel incessant, every now and then you'll notice a tiny gap between the thoughts that's open, silent, unfurnished. One thought arises and passes away, and before the next thought arises, there's a gap.

Let yourself breathe into this gap; sense it fully, and gently prolong it. For the next ten minutes or so continue to notice, sense, and prolong the gaps or pauses between thoughts in a relaxed and gentle way, and feel into the silence and stillness that these gaps reveal.

You may notice that the sense of a me disappears in the gap; that is, unlike thoughts, the gap is not self-referential, it's just open and aware. This is a glimpse of your natural state. Continue to explore the gaps from time to time as you go about your day.

However you approach this upper limit, you're on the cusp of moving beyond mindfulness into a new phase of practice. That's what this book is about; it is intended as a guide as you make the transition from mindfulness to a more natural, spontaneous, self-sustaining level of awareness. I call this level (which is actually a level beyond levels) awakened awareness, and I devote the remainder of this book to exploring it and offering you meditations and other skillful means to help you experience it for yourself.

Awakened awareness is not some new or special state of mind and heart that you need to cultivate or create, it's actually intrinsic to who you are as a human being, your natural condition, which years of conditioning have conspired to obscure.

In Buddhism and other spiritual traditions, this natural condition or state is likened to the sun, which is perpetually shining, no matter how cloudy the sky. If you want sunlight, you don't have to practice sunfulness or cultivate shining; in fact, such effort would seem ridiculous. Rather, you just need to clear away the clouds that block the light—or wait until they dissipate on their own. Similarly, once you recognize the bright sun of awakened awareness, practicing mindfulness can seem like shining a flashlight at midday in the hopes that it will make things brighter.

IN CLOSING

Mindfulness meditation has extensive, well-researched benefits. It can boost your mood, relieve your stress, improve your concentration, and increase your emotional intelligence. But it can also reinforce a subtle sense of separation between the one who's being mindful and the objects of mindfulness that can be very difficult to shake. If you aspire to wake up out of the illusion of a separate self, you may ultimately find mindfulness to be counterproductive. Instead, you can practice the direct approach described in this book, which, as its name implies, points directly to your inherent wakefulness, your natural state of awakened awareness.

I've never practiced mindfulness. Do I need to go back and practice it first before following the approach you describe in this book?

Not at all. I've framed the book as a critique of mindfulness and a guide to a more direct approach for those who may feel they've reached the limits of mindfulness. But you can also engage it directly, without preparation. As I mention in this chapter, mindfulness has many benefits and can teach you how to be present and attentive, but it also has significant limitations that may prove to be obstacles to deeper realization. Enjoy the pointers and guided meditations in these chapters and discover what they reveal for you.

You caution against using mindfulness to distance and suppress, but frankly, I have the opposite problem: I often feel overwhelmed by a sea of powerful emotions, and I can barely keep my head above water. I practice mindfulness precisely because it gives me more distance.

Yes, it sounds like mindfulness enables you to relate to your emotions without being overpowered by them. Just be aware of the pitfall of becoming addicted to your meditation practice as a refuge from difficult emotions, rather than using mindfulness to welcome them as they arise. (In chapter 7 I describe how to relate to emotions spontaneously from the perspective of awakened awareness.) If mindfulness works well for you and provides the ease and distance you seek, then by all means continue to practice and enjoy it!

You talk at great length about the limitations of mindfulness. What are the limitations of the direct approach?

Every approach has its pitfalls and limitations. Because the direct approach tends to rely on words as pointers, one risk is that you may become enthralled by the words and ignore the reality to which they point. I know many people who sound wise because they can spout the nondual jargon but have no direct experience of their natural state of awakened awareness. In the absence of a regular meditation practice to ground your attention in the present moment, you can easily get lost in the conceptual realm.

Similarly, you may confuse the emphasis on ease and effort-lessness with laziness and passivity and content yourself with the comfortable idea that awakened awareness is your natural state, without making any effort to realize it for yourself. Yes, your natural state of unconditional presence is always available to you, but until you recognize it directly, you're still stuck in the garage, as one of my teachers liked to say, and your suffering hasn't budged in the slightest.

You say it's easy for the ego to sneak into our practices and become the "one who is doing" them. But even in the practice of "just allowing everything to be as it is," isn't there room for the ego to slip in as "the one who is allowing?"

Yes, the mind can co-opt just about any practice and use it in service of its own need for control. Just as it can do a very good imitation of mindfulness, it can do an equally good imitation of allowing, without truly allowing at all. This is one of the trickiest pitfalls of the direct approach because it can be so elusive and difficult to detect. Ultimately, the mind wears itself out trying to allow and collapses back into the limitless openness that's always already allowing.

CHAPTER 2

Smuggling Donkeys

For years Nasruddin herded donkeys carrying baskets of various items back and forth across the border with the neighboring kingdom. The border guards suspected he was smuggling something, but despite their concerted searches, they could never find anything. After he retired, Nasruddin moved to a distant city and one day ran across one of the border guards at a roadside cafe. "Nasruddin," the guard greeted him, "what a surprise." After chatting for a few minutes, the guard couldn't help asking the question he'd been harboring for so many years. "Tell me, what were you smuggling?" "Ah," replied Nasruddin, sipping his tea, "I was smuggling donkeys."

Like the border guards, you have a human brain that's hardwired to ignore context and focus on content, to pay attention to the figure but neglect the ground. As you move through your day, your attention inevitably gets caught up with objects and people, with your kids, your friends, your to-do list, your colleagues at work. But do you ever stop to notice the space surrounding and infusing these objects, without which they wouldn't be able to function? Or do you take space for granted, as the invisible background in which objects appear?

Of course, space is difficult to grasp because it has no location, size, shape, or substance; it's more like the potential that makes objects possible, rather than a separate something that can be independently known. Yet you do experience space when you go to a place with an abundance of it, like a mountaintop or a beach, or when you feel its lack, as in a crowd of people or a room filled with furniture.

In a similar way, you take the screen of your computer or smartphone for granted as you become immersed in the images that play across it. Yet without this screen, as the background against which images and other information are projected, you wouldn't be able to keep in touch with the world and the people you love. Just so, you take air for granted unless you notice its lack because you're shut up in a stuffy room (or diving deep beneath the ocean's surface), even though without air you would be unable to breathe. Perhaps most important (and key to the subject of this book), you fail to pay attention to awareness, even though without it you would have no experience at all, and the world would cease to exist for you. Awareness is the neglected donkey to which the parable of Nasruddin refers.

When you practice mindfulness, you discover that awareness is a function you have the power to manipulate and control. Rather than letting it wander aimlessly and unconsciously from one object or topic to another, you can focus it deliberately, like a beam of light, from your thoughts to your physical sensations to the coming and going of your breath, and back again. As your mindfulness practice matures, your awareness builds like a muscle (or, to extend the metaphor, like a light that grows progressively brighter), your thinking mind settles down, and you reap all the wonderful benefits that awareness training confers. Rarely, however, do you meet a teacher who guides you in exploring the nature of awareness itself and invites you to take the "backward step"—the moment when you turn the light of awareness back upon itself.

DISIDENTIFYING FROM THOUGHTS AND FEELINGS

From your practice of mindfulness, you realize that your awareness is separate from your thinking; otherwise, you couldn't be aware of your thoughts. In fact, the ability to pay attention to your thinking without becoming identified with it is a key benefit of mindfulness practice that gradually frees you from the tyranny of your mind. The more time you spend noticing your thoughts, the more space or distance you have from them and the easier it gets to reflect on and respond to them in a balanced and appropriate way, rather than reacting to them in a knee-jerk fashion and reaping the consequences.

Eventually you develop what I (and others) call spacious awareness, a kind of inner openness that welcomes thoughts and feelings without being immediately identified with them. The ability to maintain spacious awareness for extended periods of time is one of the more significant stages or levels of mindfulness practice. No longer are you constantly controlled by your mind—you now have greater freedom from its dictates.

But when you practice mindfulness, you're generally taught that spacious awareness is a function you need to maintain through diligent practice. Let up on your practice, and the open window of awareness gradually closes. What if, instead, you realized that openness was not a special state that needs maintaining, but your natural state of awareness that's always present but generally obscured by the clouds of discursive thought? When you open your eyes in the morning, do you need to make an effort to be aware of your surroundings? Or is awareness immediately present and functioning as soon as you open your eyes?

MEDITATION: Entering the liminal zone

The gap between sleep and wakefulness can be a natural portal to a more expanded awareness.

When you wake in the morning, you may notice a brief period when you're between sleep and waking, when you've left the dreams of the night but haven't yet entered into the identities and plans of the day. The gap may be extremely small, but if you pay attention you can catch it and prolong it.

This gap has an unknown quality, perhaps a sense of openness and nakedness; it's a kind of liminal zone where you still don't know exactly who or what you are. You may feel afraid of this openness and tend to rush back into the known, to check your smartphone or open your computer to remind yourself who you are. Instead, just lie still and be open to the unknown.

Resist the temptation to be someone once again. Allow yourself to be no one; allow your mind to be empty of thought, unfurnished, until the identities gradually filter back in. Notice the space between your identities and the awareness of them. Notice if a similar gap appears at other times during the day, an empty space that you may have ignored before but can now lean into and prolong. Continue to open to the openness.

INTRODUCING AWAKENED AWARENESS

The distinction here may seem like a subtle one, but it has far-reaching implications. If you don't need to maintain spacious awareness, you can relax and let it happen on its own, rather than practicing it as if it were a skill. If it's self-existing and self-sustaining, you can begin to explore your relationship to it. One of the primary problems with mindfulness practice is that the mind may co-opt it and turn it into a mental observation exercise, a kind of faux mindfulness. Ultimately, this "mind full ness" becomes laborious and mechanical and undermines your innate tendency to be authentically, spontaneously present, which is the actual purpose of meditation.

MEDITATION: Letting things be as they are #1

Your natural state of inherent wakefulness, awakened awareness, welcomes reality just as it is, without resistance or grasping. You can't "do" awakened awareness, but if you follow this guided meditation, you may be able to relax back into it.

Take a few minutes to sit comfortably and shift your attention from your thinking mind to the coming and going of your breath. Now, instead of practicing your accustomed meditation technique, I'd like you to sit quietly and let everything be the way it is. Don't focus or manipulate your attention in any way, don't follow your breathing, don't *do* anything in particular; just let everything be, without trying to change or avoid or get rid of anything.

At first you may find these instructions baffling, because you're so accustomed to working with your attention. In meditation, as in life, you're adept at doing but unfamiliar with nondoing. Consider the sky—it doesn't have to do anything to include the birds and planes and other objects that pass through it. By nature, the sky is open and all-inclusive.

The same is true of your natural state of awakened awareness. Any effort to practice openness just takes you away from the innate openness of your natural state. When I say, "Just let everything be the way it is," your mind takes it as an injunction to do something special. Instead, consider it an invitation to r.est in the openness that's always already taking place.

Instead of practicing mindful attention, you can let go of any effort or manipulation and allow awareness to happen on its own. Instead of perpetuating the observing ego, you can relax into the natural observation that's always occurring. Like the sun hidden behind clouds, awareness is constantly shining; you just need to see through the layers of thoughts, beliefs, identities, and emotions that obscure it. As long as you don't cling to the old form, your mindfulness practice holds you in good stead as you progress to this next phase of awareness training. The capacity to stay present for extended periods of time, which you developed through mindfulness, can now be used to help penetrate the layers.

But why would you want to shift from the mindfulness you've been practicing for months or years and experiment with this radically different approach? Well, if you still enjoy conventional mindfulness and appreciate the many benefits it confers, perhaps you wouldn't. But if you're ready to move beyond mindfulness and experiment with a new way of being that provides lasting peace, happiness, and well-being, then you may be inclined to discover awakened awareness.

Awakened awareness isn't my invention or discovery; it's been transmitted and taught for thousands of years as the natural next step after mindfulness, indeed, as the final fruition of mindfulness. In the Buddhist tradition, from which most secular mindfulness trainings are drawn, it's called "big mind" or true self, clear light or the nature of mind, and it's considered the ultimate realization and the only abiding source of fulfillment. As I've already suggested, it differs from mindful attention in a number of significant ways. Perhaps the most important is that awakened awareness is not a state of mind; whereas mental states, no matter how exalted, come and go, awakened awareness exists prior to all passing states, as the ground of being in which all experiences arise and pass away. As I suggested earlier, it's like space or air in this regard; without it, experiences would not occur. The ground of awareness is the sine qua non in the absence of which nothing could exist. (If you're not convinced of this, imagine an experience occurring without awareness; the very notion of experience presupposes the existence of awareness.)

I use two separate terms here, *the ground of awareness* and *awakened awareness,* for a reason. At the deepest level of reality, awareness is the ground of openness in which everything arises. Whether or not you recognize it, it is always already the case. At the experiential level, however, awakened awareness does not dawn in your life until you realize that this ground of awareness is your natural state, in fact, is who you really are. This shift from recognizing awareness as a function, to recognizing awareness as the ground, to realizing it to be your fundamental nature and identity, is the awakening that the great spiritual masters describe. Only this shift can bring ultimate fulfillment, because it breaks down the illusion of being a separate person at odds with a reality out there that's constantly threatening to attack, withhold, or disappoint. As Buddha taught several millennia ago, the illusion of a separate self, and the greed, anger, and ignorance this illusion instills, is the root of all suffering. Only when you see through the illusion of separateness and realize the essential nondual nature of reality—what Zen master Thich Nhat Hanh calls our "interbeing"—can you finally reach the end of suffering and the sure heart's release.

WAKING UP FROM YOUR "ALTERED STATE"

Consciousness researchers tend to consider the levels of awareness experienced during meditation as altered states, because they require a certain effort to cultivate and maintain and they differ from the ordinary waking state of nonmeditators. But awakened awareness, as I've already indicated, is not a state in this sense because it requires no maintenance or preparation; it's always present as the background of every experience. Like the blank screen upon which images play, leaving the screen untouched and undisturbed, awakened awareness is the effortless, open space in which mind-states arise and pass away without leaving a trace.

From this perspective, most people are walking around in an altered state, that is, a state of awareness heavily altered and distorted by the accumulated stories, beliefs, memories, and experiences of a lifetime. In the words of the apostle Paul, we see life "through a glass darkly," obscured by the conditioning imposed by the mind. This conditioning filters every experience and situation through the lens of past traumas and hurts, successes and accomplishments, losses and loves, and we respond to life now not as it really is, but as we imagine it must be based on past experiences. As a result, we're never really living in the present—we're walking around in an imaginary world of our own devising, jousting like Don Quixote at windmills we take to be giants.

For example, you wake up in the morning and immediately begin to worry about the meeting with your boss you're having later in the day. Instead of enjoying the sounds of the birds at dawn or the smell of the coffee, you're off somewhere in the future anticipating what you're going to say. Based on past experiences with authority figures, you assume you're going to be reprimanded or criticized in some way, and you're already feeling fear, shame, and anger, even before you step out the door. By the time you get to work, you're extremely upset and can barely focus on the projects at hand. Nothing has happened yet—you're living in an imaginary world, an altered state fabricated by your mind, and you're seeing life through a thick veil of past conditioning.

When you penetrate this dark veil of conditioning and perceive life clearly, you leave the altered state your mind has created and return to your natural state of openness and clarity, which is your birthright as a human being. Instead of constantly reacting to imaginary slights and threats, you respond to life in the moment based on a realistic appraisal of what's really going on. And unlike the spacious awareness you cultivate in mindfulness, this openness need not be "practiced" but is always readily available and close at hand. In Zen this natural, unconditioned openness is called *beginner's mind*, and it's equated with the fully awakened awareness of the great Zen masters. Instead of cultivating it, you merely need to discover and recognize it.

Now I'm not talking about naïveté or ignorance here; you can learn from life experiences and consciously apply the lessons to your current situation—but without allowing those experiences to limit and distort your ability to be fully present and open. The difference lies in whether you're controlled by your psychological conditioning or deliberately using what you've learned to expand your possibilities. In the words of an old saying, the mind is a great servant but a poor master.

The key question is: Are you suffering or not? Ongoing psychological suffering and stress of any kind (as opposed to physical pain) are solely the province of the mind and never caused by other people or outside events or situations. If you're still struggling with life as it is, then the conditioned mind has become your master, and the most complete and enduring solution is to wake up beyond the mind to find your homeground in awakened awareness.

IN CLOSING

Like air or space, we take awareness for granted, even though without awareness the world as we know it would simply not exist. Awareness is the background of all experience, the openness in which thoughts, feelings, and sensations arise and pass away. The first step in the direct approach is to recognize that awareness is perpetually taking place, without any effort on your part. By resting in awareness knowingly, instead of trying to be mindful, you're allowing the shift from mindfulness to awakened awareness.

In the next chapter I'll describe awakened awareness in greater detail, enumerate its inherent characteristics, and show how it offers a lasting solution for all your suffering and dissatisfaction, the ultimate medicine for all your ills. In some traditions, awakened awareness is known as the wish-fulfilling jewel, the pearl of great price, that brings a dimension of peace and joy that the ups and downs of life simply can't destroy. Extravagant claims, perhaps, but such is the power and promise of the direct approach.

In the Buddhist tradition, as I understand it, mindfulness can be used as a method for achieving the deepest levels of wisdom and compassion. Why do we have to go beyond it?

30

In most traditions that point the way to spiritual awakening, mindfulness is a stepping stone, a preliminary practice that leads either to more advanced practices or to a more direct approach that invites a direct realization of our nondual nature through the use of verbal pointers and guided inquiry. For example, the author of *Mindfulness in Plain English*, the Sri Lankan monk Bhante Gunaratana, wrote a subsequent book entitled *Beyond Mindfulness in Plain English* describing the *jhanas*, progressively deeper levels of concentration and meditative absorption.

In the Vipassana tradition of Southeast Asia, mindfulness is a foundation for deeper levels of investigation and the experience of insight into the impermanent, insubstantial nature of the phenomenal world. In the Tibetan tradition, mindfulness may be followed by visualization practices, pointing-out instructions (transmitted directly from a teacher), and/or meditations designed to deconstruct the illusion of a separate self. The exercises and pointers offered in this book don't require experience in mindfulness, but regular meditation practice can provide an excellent foundation because you already know how to stay present and pay attention.

If you want to achieve the deepest levels of wisdom and compassion, you may need to go beyond mindfulness at some point. But if you're enjoying the benefits that mindfulness offers and see no reason to go beyond it, by all means keep up the practice for as long as you like. Just be aware of the pitfalls described in chapter 1, and remember that you have other options when you feel moved to explore further.

You suggest that awakened awareness is not a state but the unchanging background of all states. At the same time you say that we may leave it and then return to it. If it's not a mind-state, why does it keep changing? This sounds like a matter of semantics to me.

31

Let's go back to the analogy of the sun. On certain days in Seattle, you may not be able to tell there's a sun at all. But you know that the sun continues to shine, even though the clouds obscure it. Likewise, awakened awareness is always present and unchanging as the silent background of all experience. But it may be obscured by the clouds of discursive thought. Once you catch a glimpse of it, you have the confidence of knowing that it's always available to you when you allow the clouds to disperse. Eventually, you come to rest more consistently in unconditional openness and presence. Awakened awareness itself remains undisturbed and unchanging; the only thing that waxes and wanes is the clarity of your recognition, just as the view of the sun changes with the movement of clouds.

You seem to be implying that meditation isn't necessary to realize the deepest truth. But the great teachers in every tradition emphasize the importance of practices like meditation, prayer, and self-inquiry. Otherwise, aren't we just going to make the same mistakes over and over again?

Practices are not required, but they can certainly be helpful, even in the direct approach described in this book, as long as you engage in them as experiments or explorations designed to reveal a deeper dimension of being that's already present but not yet fully recognized. Throughout these chapters I offer direct pointers and guided meditations that invite an immediate and instantaneous realization of this deeper dimension, your natural state of awakened awareness. If, however, you practice in order to cultivate certain mind-states and achieve some future goal of enlightenment or liberation that isn't already available to you, you're just wandering away from the inherent radiance and completeness of your own being.

If you already have an intuitive grasp of awakened awareness, you may find that direct pointers are sufficient to trigger a full realization. One well-known teacher said that those who are already oriented need merely hear the instruction "Just be who you are" in order to realize their inherently awake true nature. For those who need more guidance, he suggested self-inquiry and prayer. Only you can know what practices and other skillful methods are appropriate for you. Experiment for yourself, and work with the ones that have the most resonance.

CHAPTER 3

Ultimate Medicine

Resting as unwavering awareness is the greatest of all medicines, wherein one relaxes as flawless peace that is pristine, unconditioned, and unborn, free from effort and striving, a continuous and uninterrupted equilibrium, where the eyes see without analyzing, and mind arises without reifying itself as a separate subject.

—Tibetan teacher Longchen Rabjam

Buddha is generally regarded as a pioneering spiritual teacher and the founder of one of the world's primary religions. But in his own tradition he's called the Great Physician, because he diagnosed the cause of humanity's ills and provided a solution, a remedy, a cure. You don't have to be a Buddhist or have any interest in Buddhism whatsoever to appreciate his critique of the human condition.

Despite leading a sheltered life as a prince, the future Buddha was deeply disturbed by the sickness, old age, and death he witnessed around him, and he resolved to discover a way out. After years of austerities and deep meditation, he concluded that we suffer because we crave what we can't have and resist what we have—the twin impulses of attachment and aversion. In essence, we're constantly at war with the way things are. Further, he realized that attachment, aversion, and ignorance are based on a fundamental illusion—that we're solid, separate, isolated selves living in a material world that's constantly threatening to deprive or destroy us. The only way out of this suffering, and the sure path to happiness, he discovered, was to awaken from the illusion of separation and realize our interdependence—indeed, our oneness—with all of life.

One approach to achieving this realization is to use mindfulness meditation as a powerful tool to penetrate the layers of illusion and reveal the impermanence and interdependence at the core of existence. Another approach, which emerged many centuries after the Buddha's death, is to awaken directly not only to interdependence and impermanence, but also to an abiding, all-inclusive ground of existence that is at once empty and eternal, nonlocalized and all-pervasive, infinitely spacious and deeply compassionate. When this ground of awareness reveals itself at an individual human level, it's known as consciousness, true self, Buddha nature, or awakened awareness.

Though this approach may seem abstract and amorphous, it's actually eminently practical and experiential. In other words, it works as described to provide lasting fulfillment, and the awakened awareness it points to is readily accessible, if we're ready to realize it. In this chapter, I'll bring awakened awareness down to earth and describe its principal characteristics, and I'll offer some exercises that give you an opportunity to glimpse it for yourself. The purpose is not to fill your head with spiritual jargon, but to offer direct pointers beyond suffering to your natural state of happiness and ease.

MEDITATION: Resting as awareness

This is another invitation to come to rest in the awakened awareness that's always already occurring.

Take a few minutes to sit comfortably and shift your attention from your thinking mind to the coming and going of your breath. Now, instead of practicing your accustomed meditation technique, I'd like you to sit quietly and let everything be the way it is. Don't focus or manipulate your attention in any way, don't follow your breathing, don't *do* anything in particular; just let everything be, without trying to change or avoid or get rid of anything.

Ordinarily our attention focuses on objects and interprets them, creating an inner world of meaning that has little to do with the way things actually are. Instead, let go of this grasping at objects and the tendency to judge and interpret, and relax back into awareness itself. Rest as the open, unconditional awareness in which experiences come and go. This awareness is inherently silent, present, and still; it doesn't do anything, it simply welcomes what is, just the way it is.

Let yourself rest as this silent, open, unconditional awareness or presence. No effort, no manipulation, no cultivation, no doing, just rest as awareness and let everything be as it is.

WHAT IS AWAKENED AWARENESS?

As I've already mentioned, awakened awareness, as the ever-abiding background of every experience, is self-sustaining and perpetually available. Because it's your natural state, your birthright as a human being, you don't need to cultivate or maintain it, as you do with mindfulness; you merely need to relax into it and recognize it. In fact, it's always looking through your eyes and listening through your ears, you simply fail to acknowledge it; like the space you inhabit or the air you breathe.

When you rest in (and as) awakened awareness, your habitual, conditioned way of seeing things falls away, and you experience life vividly and clearly, through fresh, unfiltered eyes and ears. Not only can this new perspective be exciting and exhilarating, it can also be a bit unsettling and disorienting, at least at first. After all, you've spent a lifetime experiencing yourself and other people in the same stale, predictable ways. Now the veils have been stripped away and you're encountering life directly, raw and unfiltered. Rarely does this new perspective become firmly established immediately. But the more you abide in this open, unconditional awareness or presence, the more you experience some of the following qualities, each of which I'll present briefly here and then explore in detail in subsequent chapters. Although I talk about them separately, these qualities or characteristics are really more like facets on a diamond than a laundry list of separate traits. Once you discover awakened awareness, they reveal themselves without effort as different aspects of a single reality.

MEDITATION: Expanding awareness beyond the body

This meditation uses direct sensate experience to release your identification with the boundaries of the physical body and open to the boundlessness of awakened awareness.

Find a quiet, comfortable place to sit for ten minutes or so. Take a few deep breaths, and allow your attention to shift from thoughts and feelings to the sensations of your body in space: the contact of your feet against the floor, your back and bottom against the chair, the coming and going of your breath.

In particular, explore the sensations at the edges of your body, where it meets your surroundings. Notice the outlines, the contours, the weight, the warmth. As you explore, notice if you can find a clear demarcation or boundary where the inside of your body leaves off and the outside world begins.

Are tactile sensations happening inside your body and sounds happening outside? Or are they all happening in the same fluid, continuous space? Are "you" somewhere inside your body, or is the experience of your body happening in you?

Now allow any remaining boundaries of your body to dissolve into the space around you. Allow this space to continue opening and expanding far beyond the boundaries of the body to include sounds, smells, objects, other people. Everything is happening in this limitless space, without edges or center.

As you allow yourself to dissolve into this space, what happens to the localized sense of being a separate someone? Where are you located? Where do you leave off and where does the outside world begin? Rest as this limitless space, without edges or center.

NO SEPARATION BETWEEN SELF AND OTHER, INSIDE AND OUTSIDE

Have you ever explored the boundaries of your body through your direct sensate experience to determine where you leave off and the outside world begins? If so, you realized that the borders are diffuse at best. Without the imposition of thought and interpretation, it's often hard to tell what is happening inside and what outside. In awakened awareness, you realize that you are the boundariless openness, the awake, aware space, in which everything arises. In other words, everything is happening in you, rather than outside you! At the same time, you don't lose sight of the fact that you're also a human being with a body encased in skin and that you need to avoid hot objects and pay attention when you're crossing the street. Both dimensions are true simultaneously.

While the ordinary, everyday sense of individuality keeps you safe at a relative level, awakened awareness reveals that you're intimately interconnected with everything else in the universe—or even more accurately, you're the space in which everything is one and inseparable. Believe it or not, it's possible to function with this limitless perspective. In fact, functioning becomes so much smoother, more harmonious, and ever so much more fulfilling when you're not constantly struggling with the world "out there." In place of fear, distrust, anger, and conflict, you now move through the world with a sense of comfort, ease, trust, and belonging. Instead of alienation or estrangement, you now feel a profound intimacy and familiarity with everything and everyone you encounter, not merely as some idea or philosophy, but as your immediate experience.

NO CENTER, NO PERIPHERY, NO SELF

As the apparent boundaries between inside and outside fall away, so too does the accustomed perspective of being a separate someone, a limited little me, centered in a particular location. If you look closely and investigate carefully, you find that the solid separate self you took yourself to be is just a shifting collection of thoughts, feelings, memories, stories, and beliefs loosely cobbled together and bound by the glue of self-referencing, that is, by the thought: *These are mine, they belong to me.* But where is the one to whom any of these thoughts belong? Where is the center to which everything apparently refers?

Awakened awareness answers this question by providing a global, expansive, all-inclusive perspective in which the apparent center drops away and everything is welcomed for what it is, without being interpreted in terms of how it benefits or threatens the separate self. Not only that, but awakened awareness confers the realization that what's looking out through these eyes and what's being looked at, the apparent subject and the apparent object, are actually just expressions of the same limitless, uninterrupted, undivided field that's inherently awake, luminous, and filled with love.

MEDITATION: Inquiring into the nature of thoughts

You may believe you know what thoughts are, but do you really? You may have been told they're the result of nerve impulses in the brain, but what is your direct experience?

Sit quietly, settle comfortably, and spend a few minutes being aware of the coming and going of your breath.

Now shift your attention to your thoughts for a few moments. Begin by noticing whether they're largely visual or auditory. In other words, do you tend to hear your thoughts, or see them, or a little of both? Do your thoughts have a color? A shape? A size? A density? Where are they located? Do they seem to be happening inside your head, or outside, or somewhere else inside your body? Where do your thoughts come from? Where do they go when they're no longer there?

Now notice that every thought refers to another thought, whether to a thought about the past or a thought about the future, a thought about others or a thought about yourself. Thoughts are constantly referring to one another, in a vast, intricate network of interrelated thoughts. Feelings form a similar self-referential network. But where is the supposedly solid, separate someone inside, to whom these thoughts and feelings refer? Can you locate it? Or is the apparent separate someone just a collection of more thoughts and feelings, constantly shifting and changing? What is your direct experience?

Now ask yourself, "Who or what is aware of these thoughts and feelings?" You're able to talk about your beliefs, your feelings, your memories, your ideas, because they are objects of your experience. Indeed, the person you generally take yourself to be is a collection of such objects. But can you find the one who is aware of them, the ultimate subject? Can the subject ever become an object of your experience?

EVERYTHING IS PERFECT AND MEANINGFUL JUST AS IT IS; THERE'S ONLY THIS

An inevitable corollary of the recognition that inside and outside are merely aspects of one undivided reality is the realization that only this moment exists. The past is just a memory and the future just a thought arising in this moment right now. If you attempt to point to something that exists outside this moment, you'll find that anything you can identify is actually presenting itself now, even your most meaningful accomplishments and cherished identities. Sure, you can list them on your résumé or post them on social media. But where do they actually exist, except as a story or a thought or an image right now? Even the present moment, when you try to catch it, can't be grasped and slips through your fingers.

Once you're thoroughly awake to the uniqueness and preciousness of this ephemeral moment, you recognize, in some mysterious way beyond your usual rational understanding, that everything that's revealing itself right now is not only unique, it's inherently complete, meaningful, and perfect, even with all its obvious imperfections. (In the words of a famous saying, it's the One without a second, and therefore beyond compare.)

These qualities have nothing whatsoever to do with dualistic polarities like complete–incomplete, perfect–imperfect, or meaningful–meaningless. Rather, every person and thing, no matter how seemingly flawed or problematic, is perfect in the sense that it simply is as it is, it couldn't possibly be otherwise, and it radiates the essential perfection of Being itself. As a natural response to this recognition there arises a subtle mix of love, wonder, gratitude, and joy. In the Judeo-Christian tradition this sense of awe at the perfection of God's creation is generally reserved for the angels, but it's actually available in the human realm through awakened awareness.

MEDITATION: Is anything missing from this moment right now?

This meditation offers an opportunity to see the world with fresh eyes, free of conceptual overlay, and catch a glimpse of the inherent perfection.

Set aside five minutes for the following exercise. First, sit quietly and rest your attention on the coming and going of your breath. Sense the rise and fall of your chest and belly as you breathe; notice the sensations of your back and legs against the chair, your feet against the floor. Be aware of the sounds around you and the sensations inside your body as well. Rest in the present moment, without effort or striving.

Now ask yourself the following question: "Without consulting the mind—that is, my thoughts, memories, beliefs, feelings, or plans—is anything missing from this moment right now?" Set aside any thoughts that might arise, and ask the question again. Can you find something that's missing or lacking that doesn't involve thought? What do you discover?

NO EFFORT, NO STRUGGLE: LIFE LIVES ITSELF THROUGH YOU

When you stop moving through life as if everything revolved around you and instead embrace each moment from the global perspective of awakened awareness as a perfect expression of Being itself, you end your constant struggle to get reality to live up to your expectations for security and comfort—and shift instead to an intuitive sense of flow with the ongoing current of life. Rather than imagining yourself to be the choreographer, you realize that you're both one of the dancers and, at a deeper level, one with the dance itself. Your role is not to impose your moves on everyone else, but to find your unique and appropriate place in the dance.

Instead of fixating on what you want and efforting to get reality to accede to your wishes, as we're taught to do from an early age in our achievement-oriented culture, you listen closely to the current of life as it flows through you and allow it to carry you where it will. Ultimately, in fact, you realize that you're not actually in control of your life at all: you're being lived by life itself. But you don't feel "out of control" because you know that you and life are inseparable, and you trust that it has its own deeper meaning and purpose that your rational mind can't comprehend.

BEING NO ONE AND SOMEONE, NOTHING AND EVERYTHING

From the global perspective of awakened awareness, you realize that you're both inseparable from everyone and everything and at the same time you're this unique body and mind moving through time and space, with your own individual preferences, abilities, and idiosyncrasies. You live at a paradoxical razor's edge of pure presence where essence emerges into manifestation, nothing flowers as everything, and no one expresses itself as someone.

Because you know that you're the space in which everything unfolds, you can't completely identify with being this little me any longer, yet you hold this person you once took yourself to be in the spacious, all-inclusive presence of who you really are with tenderness and compassion. Being someone, being nothing, and being everything are perfectly intertwined and mutually supportive (one of the great mysteries of awakened awareness). In fact, this deeper identification with the ground of being informs and infuses your thoughts and actions at every level, allowing you to flow with the current of life and giving you a profound empathy and intimacy with the experiences of everyone you meet.

TRUTH AT EVERY LEVEL; APPROPRIATE RESPONSIVENESS BASED ON THE SITUATION AT HAND

As you move through life with the clarity and compassion of awakened awareness, you discover that your commitment to the way things are is far stronger than any lingering commitment to defending old positions and points of view. As a result, you gradually drop any tendency to deceive yourself and others, no matter how subtly, and instead trust that telling the truth aligns you with the current of life, rather than setting you at odds with what is. When you're no longer centered in the contracted posturing of the imaginary self but open to the limitless expanse of awakened awareness, you naturally want what's best for the whole, rather than what's best only for the fraction. Telling the truth at every level is no longer a choice you have to make; it becomes unavoidable, like opening your eyes in the morning.

From the perspective of awakened awareness, you respond to people and situations with openness, effortlessness, and freedom from fixed points of view, and your responses are appropriate to the moment because they arise spontaneously from a full appreciation of the moment itself, rather than from the self-serving strategies of the separate self. Instead of struggling to get what you think you want, you love what life brings because you know it's exactly what's needed. As a result, your accustomed stress, struggle, frustration, and depression gradually transform into relaxation, ease, gratitude, and joy.

MYSTERY BEYOND DESCRIPTION

Beyond the words I (or anyone else) can possibly muster in some vain attempt to express the inexpressible lie the purity and inviolability of awakened awareness, our natural condition and the essence of what is. No matter how deeply you inquire, you can never plumb its depths because it can never become an object of knowledge. Rather, it is the supreme knower itself, the ultimate subject of all objects, limitless, nonlocatable, and ungraspable. You can never know it because you are it; you can only be it knowingly, that is, consciously abide *as* awakened awareness.

At the same time, because it's such a profound mystery, you can never claim awakened awareness as your possession, never own it like the other accomplishments you add to your résumé, as people sometimes imagine they can do when they're flush with the excitement of discovering it. For example, you can't say "I am awakened" and make any sense, because awakening entails the recognition that the separate someone who claims it is just an illusion. Rather, you come to realize that the person you take yourself to be, who thinks he or she can possess anything, is actually just an expression of awakened awareness, as the wave is just an expression of (and inseparable from) the ocean. Instead of the pride of achievement, the discovery of awakened awareness leads to a deepening humility and awe in the face of the mystery.

ABIDING AS AWAKENED AWARENESS

Paradoxically, then, awakened awareness is your natural state, the one who's always looking out through your eyes and listening through your ears, and at the same time it's the limitless, mysterious, ungraspable essence of what is. Indeed, this limitless essence is what you are fundamentally, the ground of your being, beneath all the dramas, roles, and identities.

Of course, these words don't mean much unless you realize for yourself the truth to which they refer. Reading that awakened awareness is your natural state doesn't bring you happiness, peace of mind, or ease of being, just as the sumptuous meals pictured on cooking websites don't satisfy your hunger. You have to learn how to approach it and knowingly abide; you need a doorway, a practice, a path that enables you to actualize it in your life and to allow it to transform you and bring you the peace and contentment you seek. But, unlike mindfulness, you can't cultivate or develop awakened awareness, because it's always already occurring; you can only recognize it, approach it, and relax into it.

IN CLOSING

In this chapter I offered a detailed description of what can never really be described, not as a catalog to be filed in your memory banks, but as a series of pointers toward the moon of awakened awareness. The hope is that the words might evoke a direct taste or glimpse—or remind you of what you already know. Unlike mindfulness, which needs to be cultivated and maintained, awakened awareness is effortlessly available in every moment. In the next chapter, I continue to point to it and offer methods for approaching it—in fact, this book is just a collection of pointers of various shapes and flavors inviting you to turn your attention back upon itself and awaken from the dream of separation once and for all.

I don't understand the point about awakening from the illusion of a separate self. I mean, I feel quite real and solid and so do the people around me. How does that cause me to suffer?

If you're convinced that you're a solid, separate person, limited to your mind and your physical body, surrounded by other equally solid, separate someones, your happiness and peace of mind depend on maintaining the survival of this separate self and on accumulating as much material and psychological well-being as you can for yourself and your family. As a result, you're constantly competing with others and struggling with the material world for what you perceive to be limited resources. You may feel contented for periods of time, but you keep lapsing back into dissatisfaction and suffering when you don't get what you want or feel you need.

If, on the other hand, you realize that the separate self is an arbitrary construct, that who you really are doesn't end with your skin, and that you're intimately interconnected with everyone and everything else, rather than competing with others, you live in a you-and-me world of love, empathy, sharing, cooperation, and mutual benefit. Your happiness and peace of mind are unshakable because you delight in the happiness of others, trust in the unfolding, and feel content with what the moment brings.

There's a wonderful story that illustrates this distinction. Imagine you're sitting at a long table with a dozen other people. You're served a sumptuous meal but your only utensils are three-foot-long chopsticks. No matter how hard you try, you can't get your food to your mouth, and you don't have the option of eating with your hands. What do you do? In one scenario, you're in a constant state of frustration and dissatisfaction as you keep trying to find a way to feed yourself. In the other scenario, you cooperate with your tablemates, reach across the table, and feed one another. When the boundaries between self and others have dissolved, caring for others means caring for yourself.

I've had periods when I was very much in touch with the inherent perfection you describe and could feel the wonder and joy. But when my husband went through chemo and could barely keep his food down, or when we lost our savings in the stock market debacle, I was just struggling to stay afloat. There was no joy there at all.

When life is going relatively smoothly, with the usual minor ups and downs, it's much easier to enjoy the perfection of the moment. But when you're faced with extreme life circumstances that appear to challenge your very survival and old conditioning kicks in or you're too exhausted to reconnect, the dream may suddenly seem quite real again. Life can be relentless. Just remember that your homeground of awakened awareness is always peaceful and undisturbed, no matter how agitated your mind may become. It's not a state that waxes and wanes like emotions, it's what abides as the ground of all states, what's left when everything else has been stripped away—comfort, faith, hope, energy, patience, optimism. Though it may feel distant, it's always close at hand—after all, it's looking out through your eyes right now—and it often rushes to the foreground to be recognized in the midst of a crisis. By all means, reconnect if you can; if not, let everything be as it is, including the frustration, anger, sadness, hopelessness, and fear. Ultimately, nothing is excluded from the nondual field of awakened awareness. (For more on connecting and reconnecting, see chapter 4. For more on relating with powerful emotions, see chapter 7.)

Is the realization of awakened awareness the same as what Zen masters call enlightenment?

The English term "enlightenment" is so fraught with cultural connotations and historical baggage that I prefer to avoid it. For example, it may convey an erroneous sense of otherworldly detachment or saintly perfection that makes it seem distant and unreachable. In many schools of Buddhism, the term "enlightenment" is reserved for the Buddha and others who abide in awakened awareness constantly, without interruption. By contrast, Zen tends to use the word more freely but still acknowledges a series of awakenings before the final breakthrough that signals the end of all seeking. I like more ordinary and accessible words like "realization" or "awakening" to refer to the recognition of awakened awareness. One of my Zen teachers used to say, there are no enlightened people, only enlightened moments. In any case, you can't claim enlightenment for yourself, because it involves the realization that there's no separate self to claim it.

Are there stages or levels beyond awakened awareness, just as awakened awareness is a level beyond mindfulness?

Actually, awakened awareness is not a level, it's your essential nature, your original face before your parents were born, the limitless, unconditional openness that's always looking out through your eyes and experiencing life through this body and mind. The realization of awakened awareness may deepen, and your ability to let go of identification and rest in it may become more stable and abiding, but awakened awareness itself never changes or lends itself to classifications of higher or lower. Beyond mindfulness lies the boundless, stageless, levelless expanse of pure awareness, pure being, without qualification.

CHAPTER 4

When Awareness Awakens to Itself

I have lived on the lip
of insanity, wanting to know reasons,
Knocking on a door. It opens:
I've been knocking from the inside.

—Jelalludin Rumi

The regular practice of mindfulness teaches you how to welcome thoughts, feelings, and other experiences without necessarily identifying with them or acting them out. By cultivating a kind of spacious awareness that does not attach to objects or experiences, you gradually become freer from the mind's conditioning. Even though habitual patterns of thinking and feeling keep arising, you don't necessarily get seduced by them.

But mindfulness alone can't offer stable, enduring peace and well-being because it's a state of mind that you believe you have to cultivate, sustain, and protect. For this reason, many mindfulness practitioners become dependent on their meditation and feel they need to return to it again and again to settle the mind down whenever it becomes agitated. Like every other mind-state, mindfulness is impermanent and arises and passes away depending on the strength and consistency of your practice. If you slack off, your mindfulness fades, and you fall back into the cauldron of negativity again.

In fact, the very notion that your mind needs to be settled and calmed or that negative emotions need to be eliminated, based on some predetermined standard of how your mind should look, marks a major distinction between the path of mindfulness and the direct approach of awakened awareness. From the perspective of unconditional openness, every thought and feeling that arises, no matter how seemingly negative or discordant, is welcomed just as it is, and this very welcoming reveals an equanimity that can't be disturbed even by the most turbulent experiences. By not preferencing one mind-state over another, so-called positive over so-called negative, awakened awareness moves beyond dualistic thinking to encompass life fully, in all its richness and complexity. Yet awakened awareness is not a state you can cultivate, but your natural state that's always already available and just needs to be acknowledged and accessed.

FREEING YOURSELF FROM THE WITNESSING TRAP

For all its wonderful benefits, the practice of mindfulness has another downside: it tends to maintain the subject–object split, the gap between the one who's being mindful, the act of being mindful, and the object of mindful attention. In other words, no matter how mindful you become, there's always a you that has to practice being mindful of an object separate from you. As a result, mindfulness perpetuates the very sense of separation it's designed to overcome. This point may be a subtle one that's not particularly relevant in the early stages of practice. But as your practice matures, you may eventually discover that you're trapped in the detached witness position and have no idea how to break free; the more you practice mindfulness, the tighter the trap becomes.

Witnessing has become another identity or point of view that you ultimately have to relinquish.

Only when you realize the awakened awareness that does not come and go but abides as the background and essence of every experience can you finally free yourself from the witnessing trap and achieve the lasting peace and happiness you seek. Awakened awareness—also known as consciousness, eternal wakefulness, pure presence, true nature, the I am—doesn't foster division because it's not separate from what it's aware of and does not prefer one experience over another. Because it exists prior to all thought or activity, it can't be created, manipulated, fabricated, or sustained; you can only recognize it, immerse yourself in it—and ultimately realize that it is what you are. Paradoxically, if you want to step into the freedom and happiness to which mindfulness points, you have to let go of the practice that mindfulness requires and let yourself fall into awakened awareness.

Unlike the cultivation of mindfulness, however, which you can learn and practice methodically, the path of discovering awakened awareness tends to be more circuitous, serendipitous, and idiosyncratic. That is, it generally differs from one individual to another and doesn't have universally applicable guideposts or milestones. Again paradoxically, it's often called the direct approach, in comparison to the progressive approach of practice and cultivation—and it's certainly direct in the sense of pointing clearly and without hesitation to the nature of mind, our natural state of awakened awareness, and inviting an instantaneous realization that requires no preamble or preparation.

At the same time, the path of discovery can be more indirect and hit-or-miss from the point of view of the seeker, who may not have the comfortable sense of progress that mindfulness affords. You may sit quietly, listen to teachings, contemplate, and inquire, yet have no sense of advancing or improving in any way—until suddenly you catch a glimpse of awakened awareness. Author

Stephen Levine calls it the "high path with no railing," because you have no landmarks or structures to support you on your way. Traditionally, the realization of awakened awareness is transmitted in person from teacher to student in intimate dialogue and exploration. For those who are interested, I offer individual and group sessions and retreats that afford this kind of intimate opportunity. But for those who are unable to avail themselves of a living teacher, the direct approach includes practices you can play with and portals or doorways that you can approach which, once opened, provide entry into a whole new way of being.

EXPERIENCING A FIGURE–GROUND SHIFT

The realization of awakened awareness generally involves a sudden, often surprising, sometimes even shocking figure–ground shift. One moment you're going about your day taking yourself to be a separate person, a locus of identity centered in the head, and the next moment you recognize that you're the vast openness in which this apparently separate person and every other object of experience occur. From thinking of yourself as a body–mind with a personal history and an imagined future localized here, you realize that you're this insubstantial but all-pervasive awareness in which life unfolds in some mysterious and ungraspable way. The center of your universe has shifted dramatically—in fact, you may have lost your center entirely—and you can never quite return to your old way of experiencing life again.

Though this shift may sound like a mystical experience, a glimpse of another, more spiritual dimension of reality, it's actually a profound insight beyond the veil into the nature of reality itself. Just as scientists over the centuries have used the scientific method of objective experimentation to gradually unlock the secrets of the physical universe, so have meditators, yoga practitioners, and sages used a similarly scientific method of subjective investigation to discover the metaphysical ground of existence. Like experiments in physics and chemistry, these exercises and meditations have reproducible results, though some may prove more effective for a particular individual than others. Choose the ones that seem to work best for you, follow them carefully and wholeheartedly, and you'll eventually realize what the great masters have realized before you. In this chapter, I offer experiments and pointers you can implement for yourself.

PASSING THROUGH THE GATELESS GATE

At the heart of the direct approach lies a paradox: How can you possibly become what you already are? If awakened awareness already exists as your natural state and can't be cultivated or practiced, why must you approach or become it in any way at all? Why not just be it? Well, the fact is that you already are it, at least intrinsically, yet you continue to suffer because you don't consciously recognize what you are. Clearly you need to do something, change your point of view in some way, to be able to align yourself with what's already the case. That is, you need to be it knowingly—awareness has to awaken to itself.

In Zen, this paradox, of being it but not recognizing it, is known as the gateless gate. You find yourself outside a gate that appears to separate you from the fundamental truth at the heart of reality, and you try every possible method to break through. When you finally reach the other side and discover what you were trying so hard to achieve, you realize that the gate was just a figment of your imagination, and you were never outside of it even for an instant. But without the exploration and investigation, the sitting and inquiring, you may never have recognized that the gate didn't exist.

None of the descriptions and explanations I offer can crack this paradox for you; only direct, immediate experience will do the trick. The exercises in this chapter invite you to enter the gateless gate for yourself.

WELCOMING WHAT IS

Since awakened awareness has no opinions for or against anything and welcomes everything just as it is, without judgment or interpretation, you can approach it by sitting quietly and opening to reality in a welcoming, nonjudgmental way. The risk of this approach is that the mind, a consummate mimic, can do an excellent imitation of welcoming and appear to be unconditionally open, while actually harboring judgments and maintaining a limited point of view. The secret is to stop controlling your attention and allow it to function effortlessly, without the intervention of the mind. In a sense, you have to fail as a mindful meditator in order to go beyond mindfulness; that is, your mindfulness has to give way and spontaneously open to reveal the unconditional openness prior to mindfulness. Any attempt to "do welcoming" is doomed to be a dead end that leaves you stuck in efforting and has nothing to do with unconditional, unlimited openness.

If this undertaking sounds tricky, subtle, and (once again) paradoxical, you're on the right track. As Lao Tzu, the great sage of the *Tao Te Ching*, advises, you have to learn how to "do nondoing" for awakened awareness to flower. But sitting quietly can invite this shift to nondoing, as long as you let go of your habitual attempts to get somewhere or accomplish something by cultivating a particular state, even if it's greater presence and peace of mind. (As you may have noticed, when you're efforting to get your mind to settle down, you're just stirring the waters and causing more turmoil.) Let go of your mindfulness and just be. (For instructions in just being, see chapter 3.)

MIND LIKE THE SKY

As I mentioned in a previous chapter, your natural state of open, awake, unconditional awareness is like the sky—it doesn't have to effort or try in any way to welcome everything without judgment or discrimination in its limitless embrace. Welcoming is the spontaneous and effortless nature of the sky. Planes, birds, skydivers, and balloons don't need to ask the sky to open and allow them to pass through. Permission has always already been granted, and the sky just receives them without being disturbed in any way.

Likewise, when you let go of your effort to be mindful, you can sit quietly and imagine that you are the sky, without center or boundaries. Thoughts, feelings, images, memories, and judgments come and go in the boundless presence of awakened awareness— which is what you are fundamentally. Everything is happening in you! As your understanding deepens, you shift from practicing mindfulness, to cultivating spacious awareness, to resting in openness, to realizing that this skylike openness is your very own true nature. The final realization that you are the openness, the boundariless space, and at the same time you're inseparable from what arises in this space, marks the full flowering of awakened awareness.

MEDITATION: Resting as global awareness

Most of the time our awareness is contracted and fixated on particular objects. But awakened awareness is all-inclusive, like the sky.

Take a few minutes to sit comfortably and shift your attention from your thinking mind to the coming and going of your breath. Now, instead of practicing your accustomed meditation technique, I'd like you to sit quietly and let everything be the way it is. Don't focus or manipulate your attention in any way, don't follow your breathing, don't *do* anything in particular; just let everything be, without trying to change or avoid or get rid of anything.

Let yourself rest as this silent, open, unconditional awareness or presence for five minutes or so. No effort, no manipulation, no cultivation, no doing, just rest as awareness and let everything be as it is.

Now imagine the space directly in front of your body. Objects in front in no way interfere with this space. Feel into this space; as you breathe, allow your awareness to expand to include this space.

Now imagine the space directly behind your body. Objects behind in no way interfere. Feel into this space; as you breathe, allow your awareness to expand to include this space.

Now do the same with the space to the right of your body, the space to the left of your body, the space above your body, and the space below your body. Sense this spacious, global openness in every direction. Is it conscious or unconscious? Does it have any limits or boundaries? Does it have a center? Where does it begin and where does it leave off? Does it reject or hold onto anything?

Remain as this global openness—limitless, unattached, all-inclusive, like the sky.

CONTEMPLATING DIRECT POINTERS

Another powerful doorway to awakened awareness involves contemplating the direct teachings of the great sages from every tradition who have intimately understood and lived it. These teachings are sometimes called pointing-out instructions because they direct awareness back upon itself to discover who or what is being aware—that is, awakened awareness. If you're especially fortunate, you may actually hear these words from the lips of a living teacher. If not, you may stumble upon pointing-out instructions in books and find yourself spontaneously responding to their invitation.

In my own case, I met a teacher who told me, "The seeker is the sought. The looker is what he or she is looking for." This dictum resonated deep inside and initiated a kind of spontaneous wondering, as pointing-out instructions often do. But it was months before it bore fruit in a sudden, enlightening moment of insight into its deeper significance.

If you want to reap the wisdom of these pointers and don't have a living teacher you can visit in person, you can find excellent instructions online or in books. The secret is to avoid teachings that fill your mind with information and interpretation, and instead to gravitate to those that point directly to awakened awareness: the timeless presence beyond the mind. In Zen, these direct pointers are known as turning words, because they turn the mind toward the truth. They're also called live words, because they're infused with the vibrant energy of their source, as opposed to the dead words that just convey thoughts and concepts. *Koans*, the enigmatic stories that Zen students contemplate and endeavor to resolve, often culminate in a turning phrase, though many use a kind of Zen jargon that makes them difficult to decipher. Classic turning phrases arise spontaneously in the moment in response to a student's core question and are uniquely suited to the situation and the needs of the questioner.

INQUIRING INTO THE ONE WHO IS AWARE

In addition to contemplating the direct pointers of others, you can actively inquire into the nature of the one who is aware. The classic approach is to ask some variant of the question "Who am I?" with the understanding that the usual answers—for example, I'm a woman, a dancer, a teacher, a father, an entrepreneur, a meditator, a Christian, a tennis player, an artist—are not who you really are. The point is to direct attention beyond all the stories, roles, and identities you've accumulated over a lifetime to arrive at who you are essentially, prior to your life history and condition-ing. In Zen, they call this fundamental, essential nature your "original face before your parents were born." For the purposes of this book, we call it awakened awareness.

For many people, the question "Who am I?" is too abstract and doesn't have any resonance or traction. If so, you can use something more concrete and experience-near, like "Who is experiencing this moment right now?" or "Who is looking out through these eyes right now?" The purpose is not to engage the logical, deductive mind but to ask a question that goes to the heart of the matter directly and elicits a resolution through another, more unmediated way of knowing. You need to ask the question with your whole being and let it resonate energetically, throughout your body, as if you were dropping a pebble into a pond and allowing the ripples to radiate out unimpeded. Eventually the answer reveals itself in a way that you couldn't pos-sibly have anticipated.

BE AWARE OF WHAT YOU'RE NOT;
REST IN WHAT YOU ARE

Instead of asking "Who am I?" or one of its variants, you can contemplate the following penetrating riddles or paradoxes, which inevitably point in the same direction. Again, don't waste your time trying to figure them out with your rational, analytical mind. Instead, let them resonate deeply and elicit an answer from another level of knowing, beyond the mind. As with self-inquiry, the answer doesn't arrive in a neat conceptual package, the way thoughts do; rather, it overtakes you and dawns on you as a profound, life-changing insight or intuition.

- Throughout your life you have used your name and the pronoun "I" to refer to yourself, even though you're a completely different person than you were ten, twenty, thirty, or forty years ago. The cells in your body have died and been replaced multiple times, your body bears little resemblance to the body you had when you were five or ten, your thoughts and feelings are totally fresh and new, and your inner narrative is changing constantly. Yet you have an intuitive sense of something that has remained unchanged over the years, to which the word "I" refers. Where is this abiding, unchanging "I"?

- Anything you can experience is an object of your awareness. When you say "I see a tree" or "I hear a bird" or "I know a fact," the bird, fact, or tree is an object, and "I" is the subject. For this reason, you can never know or experience the I, because as soon as you think you've grasped it and turned it into an object, it's eluded your grasp. "I" is the ultimate subject of all objects, but can never become an object of experience or knowing itself. Yet it can be known in a more direct way that does not pass through the mind and the process of objective knowing. Who is this I?

- Everything you experience is not what you are fundamentally. The thoughts, feelings, sensations, memories, beliefs, images, and stories you generally take to be you are merely objects of your attention and can't be what you really are. But when you're aware of what you're not—body, senses, mind—you rest in what you are. What is it?

YOU ARE THE PATH

Ultimately, there's no predetermined path or methodology for discovering who you are fundamentally, your homeground of awakened awareness, because no one can possibly know what questions, meditations, and explorations will resonate for you and unlock your gateless gate. Traditional teachings recommend sitting quietly, listening to the words of an awakened teacher, contemplating the teachings, inquiring for yourself, and associating with others on a similar path. But you need to find what works for you by becoming intimately attuned to your own inner knowing and getting an intuitive sense of when you're getting closer and when you're wandering away. This kind of deeper resonance is difficult to teach and generally only emerges gradually as you orient to the truth these teachings convey.

In this chapter, I've offered a number of meditations and explorations, but they're not intended to be a systematic practice.

Find the ones that appeal to you most and engage in them whole-heartedly, but don't expect particular results, as that will bias any discoveries you might make. Keep the freshness of "beginner's mind," and you'll eventually realize awakened awareness for yourself. After all, beginner's mind and awakened awareness are one and the same!

In a similar way, the pointers and descriptions presented in this book are not intended as answers but as hypotheses you need to prove or disprove. For example, you've been told that awakened awareness is your natural state, prior to thought, that it's always available to you, and that it's the ultimate source of lasting peace, happiness, and love. But do you really know the truth of these statements for yourself? Until you do, everything in this book is nothing but talk.

With a regular practice like mindfulness, you have the comfort of knowing that you're doing something with well-researched benefits that seem to apply more or less equally to everyone. But as I mentioned earlier, the direct approach is more idiosyncratic. Trust your intuition, be sincere and diligent in your experimentation, and be a lamp unto yourself, as the Buddha advised.

IN CLOSING: JUST BE WHO YOU ARE

If you're adventurous, you can try the most direct approach of all, which is also the most elusive and precarious: Just be who you are. Don't bother with the methods presented in this chapter, let go of all attempts to manipulate your attention in any way, and rest as unconditional openness without preamble, preparation, or practice. Awakened awareness is the eternal, undisturbed, unchanging backdrop of all experience; it's the light behind all perceptions, the ultimate subject of all objects, the blank screen on which the apparent phenomenal world is projected, the nondual field in which life unfolds. You can't practice, do, or cultivate it in any way. Instead, just *be* it.

When I try to let go, as you suggest, I just get tied up in knots and end up feeling more tense and stressed out than when I started. Am I doing something wrong?

The paradox, of course, is that you can't do letting go, you can only allow it. As long as you're trying to "do" it, you're not really letting go, you're holding on to your trying. Stop trying, and letting go happens by itself. It's like releasing a ball that you've been gripping so tightly: Don't let go, just stop holding on, and the ball falls from your hand. Sometimes, simply noticing that you're holding on spontaneously triggers a letting go. After all, relaxation and ease are your natural condition, your default mode, before a lifetime of conditioning taught you that you had to maintain control to survive.

I'm not sure I trust myself well enough to be a lamp unto myself and intuit my own direction, as you suggest. After all, my judgment hasn't been very reliable in the past; that's why I started mindfulness practice.

Perhaps mindful attention to your experience from moment to moment has enabled you to become more attuned to your own inner, intuitive knowing, the place beyond analysis or judgment where you sense what's best for you. For example, how did you choose a career or a partner, or what book to read next, or whom to befriend? How do you know what foods to eat when? You're constantly consulting an inner GPS to guide you through life, and the process of recognizing your true nature is no different. In the end, only you can know what's best for you; no one else, not even the wisest teacher, can be an authority on your path to awakened awareness. Of course, expert counsel from an experienced teacher can be invaluable, and there are countless teachings available these days to point you on your way. But ultimately you have to discern which guidance to follow.

CHAPTER 5

Practicing the Direct Approach

When you allow yourself to rest as unconditional openness,
you're permeated and infused with the fullness of being,
which expresses itself through the heart as qualities like
wonder, gratitude, joy, luminosity, and love.

With the realization of awakened awareness, your experience of life dramatically changes: From imagining yourself to be a collection of thoughts, feelings, memories, and stories located somewhere inside your body, usually the head, you shift to recognizing yourself as the limitless openness in which the body–mind and every other object appears. Like the cognitive shift that occurs with one of those figure–ground puzzles you studied in psych class, once you see who you really are, that is, the field of awareness in which the world of objective reality reveals itself, it's impossible to look at yourself in the same way ever again. You've awakened from a dream, and you can't pretend to unsee what you've already seen.

At the same time, you may keep straying away from the truth that you've discovered and falling back to sleep. The pull of the small mind, the ego, is so strong that it keeps resuscitating itself and drawing you back into the old pattern of taking yourself to be your story rather than the one who is aware of (and beyond) the story. In other words, you mistake yourself for an object, even though you know that you're the ultimate subject. After realization, the practice is not about trying to see something you haven't already seen, but about returning and abiding in the truth you know yourself to be. If sitting quietly or inquiring, as you did before, helps bring you home to awakened awareness, then by all means practice these, just as long as you remember that you're not trying to cultivate a state you don't already have or get someplace you don't already inhabit. Awakened awareness is your nearest, as close to you as breath, as intimate as opening your eyes and gazing out at the world as if for the first time.

As in mindfulness practice, each moment of practicing awakened awareness offers a choice-point: Do I allow myself to become distracted and get seduced back into the drama? Or do I choose the openness, clarity, disidentification, and freedom that I discovered but keep forgetting? The difference is that with mindfulness you keep choosing to be aware, whereas with the direct approach you keep reminding yourself that you are awareness itself. This is the meaning of awakened awareness—awareness that consciously and deliberately rests as itself, without attaching to objects or outcomes. (One of my first Zen teachers used to describe this as "settling the self on the self with imperturbability.") At once subtle and profound, this distinction marks the boundary between the direct and progressive approaches. (For more on this distinction, see chapter 1.) In mindfulness, the emphasis is on objects of awareness; in the direct approach the emphasis is on the ultimate subject: awakened awareness itself. Having located your (paradoxically boundariless and nonlocatable) homeground, you keep returning home, again and again. In essence, you're practicing being what you already are, which is (once again) paradoxical and makes no sense to the rational mind.

MEDITATION: Letting things be as they are #2

Once you discover awakened awareness, you can keep returning directly when you sit in meditation, rather than practicing some technique to get you there. Admittedly, this is an advanced practice, but at a certain point, as your understanding deepens, you can come home directly without detours.

Begin by sitting quietly and being aware of the coming and going of your breath for a few minutes. Now just let everything be as it is, without effort or manipulation. Even the idea of being open is a kind of effort or manipulation, at this stage, so let go even of the attempt to be open and allow everything to be the way it is. This is the fundamental sitting instruction: Let it be. Letting it be is the ultimate openness; it's an allowing rather than a doing of any kind.

As thoughts and feelings come and go, don't try to change, avoid, attach to, or get rid of them. Just let them be. By letting them be, you abide in the openness of awakened awareness. Your homeground is always open and free of what it's aware of, and by being aware of objects without getting caught up in them, you rest in being awareness, the ultimate subject of all objects.

Again, the difference between the choiceless awareness of the mindfulness tradition and awakened awareness is subtle but crucial: With choiceless awareness, the emphasis is still on the objects of awareness, allowing attention to move freely and spontaneously from one object to another. With letting it be, you're consciously resting as the subject, awareness itself, and allowing objects to do what they do without focusing on them in any way. Like the sky, you're free of what passes through it. Like a mirror, you're undisturbed by what's reflected in it. This is the nature of awakened awareness.

ABIDING IN THE FULLNESS OF BEING

At a practical level, awakened awareness has an experiential, energetic dimension. When you allow yourself to rest as unconditional openness, you're permeated and infused with the fullness of being, which expresses itself through the heart as some of the qualities I enumerated in earlier chapters: comfort, ease, trust, belonging, wonder, gratitude, joy, luminosity, love. Though we use different words and concepts to describe what seem to be differing qualities, in fact these are just facets of the jewel of awakened awareness as it's experienced on the physical or energetic level. Unlike in mindfulness, you don't need to make an effort to cultivate these qualities; they just naturally arise when you rest in the fullness and openness of awakened awareness.

For this reason, abiding as awareness is the core practice (if we can call it a practice) that follows on the realization of awakened awareness. Just be who you are! By abiding in this way, you allow the fullness of being to express itself through you without any intervention or manipulation on your part. In your body you inevitably experience this fullness as an infinite expansiveness that embraces everything and every possibility, a kind of passionate and all-inclusive yes to life as it is. Some teachers use words like inspiration (infused with spirit) or enthusiasm (filled with

God) to describe this open, expanded, compassionate space. It's as if you've aligned yourself with the natural flow of the universe and feel like you're being carried along and aloft by its energy. Of course, these are all just concepts until you arrive at the experience to which they point.

Once you become familiar with this energetic expansion and fullness, you can keep returning to it directly, from moment to moment, without using any intermediary practices. Just keep flashing on the openness/fullness and rest there.

MEDITATION: Abiding in the fullness of being

As you become more accustomed to letting go and letting be, you begin to experience the fullness of being as an energetic experience, as described in the previous section. Like a jewel, this experience is extremely rich, luminous, and multifaceted, and it's ultimately without an experiencer, because when you find yourself in the fullness of being, the sense of being a separate someone experiencing something has already fallen away.

Throughout the day, you can keep returning to the experience of the fullness of being, flashing on it for a few moments, then returning to whatever you're doing. Again, this has nothing to do with being mindful; it's more like a dissolving into the current of love, gratitude, and joy that permeates existence. This current can't be taught or described; because it's the essence of what is, it can only be pointed out. But once you stumble upon it, you'll recognize it immediately, just as the Prodigal Son recognized his long-lost home.

In some traditions, this indescribable essence is known as the wish-fulfilling jewel, the nectar of the gods, the ultimate medicine for all our ills. Abide in it and allow it to permeate your body and mind, and you'll find that it's profoundly healing at every level.

RETURNING HOME WHEN YOU WANDER OFF

"All well and good," you may wonder, "but how can I return home and abide when I've wandered away from the truth of my being? As soon as I feel like I've lost my ground, I start anxiously struggling to regain it and end up drifting farther and farther away. At this point, the directive to just be who I am or to rest and abide means absolutely nothing to me." The key here is to remember that you haven't lost anything: What you are looking for and trying so hard to grasp is what is looking; the seeker is what is being sought. Instead of searching outside yourself in an attempt to reproduce some special state of mind as if it were an object you could recapture, simply sit quietly once again and allow everything to be as it is. Through this allowing, in which you're completely unattached to any state of mind, including being the ground of awareness, you immediately (and paradoxically) return to the ground you thought you'd lost but which was in fact always already available to you. In the words of one great master, "Let go of it, and it fills your hand."

Alternatively, you can flash on the question "Who am I?" (or whatever form of inquiry has resonance for you) and instantaneously reconnect with your homeground, without foraging around in your mind looking for answers. Or you can recall a brief pointer or teaching phrase that immediately beckons you home. Become familiar with what works for you—and when it stops working, experiment until you find something that does. The more you keep returning to rest as awareness, the easier and quicker the path home becomes. Eventually, you only need to click your heels and remind yourself that there's no place like home, like Dorothy in *The Wizard of Oz*, to find yourself in Kansas again! That is, the return occurs spontaneously and instantaneously, moment after moment, until you never leave home again. Just remember that what you're returning to has no location or substance, it isn't an object or thing, it's the unconditioned, ungraspable openness in which the apparent separation between inside and outside, self and other, has dropped away and everything unfolds freely just as it is.

WAKING UP AGAIN AND AGAIN

Of course, living in such unconditional openness and fullness of being, free from fixed identities and agendas, can seem challenging and disorienting at first, especially since the culture, the people around you, and your own conditioning collude to seduce you into identifying with being a particular separate person again. Each of us lives in a dream world of our own creation that we take to be reality. The story of me is a drama filled with heroes and villains, successes and failures, gains and losses, that's usually marked by struggle and conflict and has the separate self at its center. Discovering yourself as awakened awareness means waking up from this dream to the fullness of life as it is, right now, in this timeless moment, free of the limitations that your ideas, interpretations, and stories impose. But the dream is so familiar, and the other dream characters so attached to your engagement in the dream, that you keep getting sucked back in again and again.

At this point, the key to abiding in awakened awareness is to clarify once and for all where home really lies and then to keep reminding yourself to return. Habitual patterns of thinking, feeling, and responding and the comfortable, self-fulfilling story you weave about yourself can seem as familiar and homey as a well-worn shoe. But is it who you really are or where you really abide, at the deepest level? If you opt for comfort and familiarity over the clarity and freedom of awakened awareness, you'll wander endlessly through the hills and valleys of conditioned existence, the roller-coaster ride of birth and death; what the Buddhists call *samsara*. You need to be convinced that you can't find lasting fulfillment there.

For example, you may take great pride in your accomplishments—the difficulties you've overcome, the relationships you've cultivated, the places you've visited, the money you've made. But the memories of even the best past experiences can crowd your mind and prevent you from being fully present right now and appreciating the joy and fulfillment that this irreplaceable moment potentially affords. Or you may find yourself gravitating back with sadness and shame to your failures, your lost opportunities, your mistakes, the people you've hurt, the traumas you've suffered. But this haze of negative thoughts and feelings keeps you from having more positive experiences now that might help alleviate your pain. Or you may keep recycling the story of how you've been wronged, abandoned, or overlooked by others, and your resentment has embittered you and cut you off from the love that's available to you now. You may suffer because you compare your present experiences unfavorably with those you've had in the past or live in constant fear that the same traumas and disappointment that befell you before will happen again. And your relationships are never really fulfilling because they're clouded by judgments, expectations, projections, and the shadow of previous heartache and loss. Wandering endlessly in the story of your life, you suffer because you've separated yourself from, and can't genuinely connect with, life as it is.

MEDITATION: Getting to know
the dream you inhabit

As a first step in the process of awakening, you can become intimately familiar with the dream you're longing to awaken from and recognize that it's not who you are.

For the next week, pay special attention to the dream you're constantly weaving about yourself. Make it an object of your investigation, as you would a mystery you're trying to solve. Notice the stories you tell yourself about other people in your life and how they figure into your narrative. Who are the villains, and who are the heroes? Do you tend to make yourself right and other people wrong? Or do you beat yourself up for all the mistakes you believe you're making?

Notice the feeling tone of the dream—the anger, the fear, the hurt, the shame. What are the recurring themes and issues? Where did you learn to see life in this way?

Notice that sometimes the stories seem to recede into the background and loosen their grip. How do you feel then? What happened to the stories? Remember that the stories you tell yourself about reality generally have very little to do with what's actually going on. They're interpretations, projections onto the blank screen of possibility, which then have a powerful effect on what actually happens.

What would it be like to live free of your stories? How would you feel? What would your life be like? If you're not the dream or the dream character, who are you?

TAKING REFUGE IN AWAKENED AWARENESS

The recognition that the separate self is a setup for suffering may well have motivated you to seek awakening in the first place. As a reminder of your commitment to staying awake, you may find it helpful to return to this recognition again and again, just as periodically putting your finger to a hot stove confirms that it does indeed still have the power to burn. If you don't, life does an excellent job of reminding you, by offering up situations where your attachment to a fixed position or agenda, a self-image or story, or a habitual pattern of reacting elicits familiar painful feelings of anger, fear, defensiveness, or hurt. When you suddenly find yourself suffering again, take it as a wake-up call to remember your true home and return on the spot.

In the Buddhist tradition, this constant returning to your homeground of awakened awareness is known as taking refuge from the suffering of conditioned existence. Once you awaken, you can no longer take refuge in the dream; you've been forcibly disillusioned. Though you may keep wandering back for a visit, you can't set up your headquarters there. Indeed, your sojourns back to the dream may be even more painful than before and the feedback loop quicker and shorter. As a result, you may feel like your suffering has grown more intense since you realized yourself to be awakened awareness, because every time you get close to the stove you get burned.

The good news is that your commitment to realizing the truth of your being has borne fruit and now conspires to bring you home again and again. Indeed this commitment involves a kind of renunciation, not of the material comforts or intimate relationships that a monk or nun might renounce, but of the attachment to the dream world you've created. Commitment, refuge, and renunciation comprise three aspects of the movement toward truth. Renouncing the conventional belief that you can find true happiness and fulfillment in the dream, you take refuge in awakened awareness and commit yourself to living from this understanding as consistently as possible.

MEDITATION: Keeping it in front of you

Because your natural state of unconditional presence is the background of all experience, you can practice allowing thoughts and feelings to unfold in front of you like a film playing itself out before your eyes. You are the light behind the film that makes the images possible; you can't be found among the cast of characters. At the same time, paradoxically, the character you generally take to be you continues to play its part in the film.

In sitting meditation, you can practice being the sky in which thoughts and feelings arise like clouds (as described in the previous chapter). The sky welcomes but does not involve itself in what arises.

As you move through everyday life, you can stop from time to time and rest as awakened awareness—that is, awareness that rests knowingly in itself—as you allow life to unfold like a dream without interfering. This noninterference doesn't mean being passive but includes not interfering with the flow of your own actions as well. The Taoists call this "doing nondoing," or effortless activity without a center or doer. You interact within the dream as much as you feel moved to do, but you're not identified with the drama or attached to the outcome. You're balanced at the razor's edge between being no one and being someone, nothing and everything.

If none of this makes any sense to you, don't worry. Just set it aside and experiment with the practices that have resonance for you.

GOING TO PIECES WITHOUT FALLING APART

When your locus of identity shifts from the dream character to awakened awareness, you may have the disconcerting feeling that your life as you knew it is falling apart, and you may find yourself scurrying to put the pieces back together again, like Humpty Dumpty's companions in the nursery rhyme. Expressions like "pull yourself together" and "have your ducks in a row" betray the meme that you need to stay in control of every aspect of your life if you're going to survive in a difficult world.

But the realization of awakened awareness reveals a deeper and more mysterious order at the heart of existence that doesn't center on you as a separate person but instead finds expression in the inherent wholeness and perfection of life as it is. In the words of one Zen master, "Everything is perfectly managed in the unborn," that is, there's an implicate order that takes care of everything and allows you to let go of the illusion of being in charge. For a careful investigation shows that control is just that, an illusion. Do you control the beating of your heart, or the functioning of your internal organs, or your breathing most of the time? Can you control the flow of your thoughts and feelings? Are you even in control of your actions? In fact, brain research demonstrates that the decision to move your arm or get a bite to eat comes a split-second after the impulse to act has actually occurred.

At an everyday level you may have the impression that you can micromanage your life—until you can't anymore because life circumstances, unforeseen events, or physical, psychological, or material limitations prevent you. But when you realize awakened awareness, you're forcibly dislodged from the apparent center of your life and shifted to the background, if only for a moment or two, as life unfolds before and within you in its own mysterious way. Suddenly you release your tight grip on life and discover that it was completely unnecessary. You thought you were navigating the car, when all along you were a little child tightly gripping a toy steering wheel as Mom or Dad—God, the mystery, the implicate order—did the actual driving.

As a result of dropping the illusion of control, you may no longer have the same drive (or, perhaps more accurately, no longer feel driven) and no longer find the same meaning in life. In fact, the collapse of the dream has brought a corresponding collapse in the personal meaning that the dream projected. The prevailing dream in the West is based on the myth of the hero, the powerful person in charge of his or her life who finds ultimate meaning by overcoming obstacles and fighting against the odds to win the prize, reach the finish line, succeed at some Herculean task. We idolize people who live out some version of this myth—the aging swimmer who overcomes the elements to make it across a shark-infested body of water, the poor kid who works his way to the top of a big corporation, the young girl who sails solo around the world despite bad weather and equipment failure. (The popularity of superhero movies attests to the fascination with this meme.) Needless to say, the hero dream places the emphasis on the separation between the individual and the rest of reality—it's a dream of struggle, conflict, and ultimate triumph.

Even if you don't fancy yourself a hero, you're still probably judging yourself by some version of this fundamental standard. Indeed, the ego inevitably takes itself to be the hero of its own story and finds value in how well it succeeds—at making a living, finding a mate, winning love and approval. But when you realize that you're no longer the separate center around which your life revolves but just another expression of the greater movement and flow of life itself, the hero dream and the world of personal meaning you've constructed around it collapses. Now what? If the meaning of your life is not founded in personal significance and success, what's the point?

Instead of struggling to reconstruct the dream and the meaning it provided, which is doomed to failure in any case, you can keep returning to your homeground of awakened awareness and find ultimate meaning there. When you let go of the effort to make life happen and instead abide as unconditional openness and presence without a center, you realize that nothing extra needs to be added to this moment to make it more complete—it's inherently perfect and meaningful just as it is. By going to pieces as a separate self, you've discovered the deeper ground of the undivided, the one without a second, the eternal source from which all apparent separation arises. Once you realize your identity with this deeper ground of being, the search for personal meaning naturally comes to an end.

IN CLOSING

There's no way to practice or maintain awakened awareness, as you might do with a state like mindfulness. But once you recognize it to be your very essence, your true nature, your natural state, you can keep noticing your tendency to wander off into identification and keep returning to abide as what you know yourself to be. In the words of one great Indian sage, "You merely need to find out your source and take up your headquarters there." As the habit of identifying with the mind drops away, so does the need to control or manipulate life to live up to your expectations, and you naturally open to the inherent completeness and perfection of every moment, just as it is.

I've always tried to live a "purpose-driven life" and do what I believe to be meaningful to me. Now you're suggesting that the drive to find personal meaning is misguided. Does this mean that I've been wasting my time all these years?

I wouldn't say that you've been misguided, because what you've been doing has brought you to the point of questioning your approach and inquiring more deeply. Within the dream of being a separate person with a life history, an anticipated future, certain goals and expectations, and a desire to have an impact and exert some control, choosing to pursue a personal sense of purpose makes complete sense. But the drive to impose your agenda, however lofty the purpose, blinds you to what's actually needed and sets you at odds with the natural flow and direction of life, which has its own intrinsic meaning. The emptier you are of purpose and preconceptions and the more open to listening to what life has to offer, rather than to your ideas about how things should be, the more meaningful life becomes, and the better able you are to respond appropriately to the moment and to be of genuine benefit. Resting in awakened awareness involves an intimate, global listening to the whole situation just as it is, then allowing your purpose to arise spontaneously in alignment with the situation at hand—and to shift and change with the flow.

I find it hard to believe that "everything is perfectly managed in the unborn," as you maintain. Look at all the violence, ignorance, and greed in the world, all the wars, the terrorist attacks, the environmental depredation. Reality doesn't seem perfectly orchestrated to me!

How can you know that the wars, terrorist attacks, and environmental depredation aren't absolutely what needs to happen according to some mysterious order that your mind can't comprehend? Do you suppose that you or anyone else on the planet knows what's best for the whole? Remember that the perfection I'm referring to has nothing to do with the opposites of perfect or imperfect, good or bad. Rather, it's perfect in the sense that it couldn't possibly be otherwise—it's what's meant to happen. And how do you know that? Because it does! Otherwise, you're constantly at odds with reality, which, as one of my teachers used to say, makes you a loser only 100% of the time.

Of course, if you feel moved to make changes or join with others to protest the status quo, by all means do so—your response to life is part of the perfection as well. But don't be attached to the results, or you'll be endlessly frustrated and disappointed. Reality moves in its own mysterious, ineluctable, and—dare I say it—perfect way, whether you like it or not. You can choose to let go of your struggle and separation and relax into your natural state of awakened awareness, which is inherently at one with the flow. Or you can wear yourself out with resistance against the way things are. Again, when you're immersed in the flow, you're not necessarily passive, but your responses are appropriate to the situation at hand.

I know I'm not my body, my story, or my personality, but I've never had any of the energetic experiences you describe. It's more of a simple insight or recognition of what's true.

The initial realization will often take the form of a simple insight. As it permeates your being and reaches your heart, it will flower as the energetic experiences of love, gratitude, and the other qualities I describe. The main thing is that you have a clear and unarguable recognition of the nondual fabric of reality with your whole being, not just as some worldview you understand with your mind. In the Western religious traditions, this direct apperception beyond the mind is called *gnosis*; in the East it's known as *jnana* or *prajna*. It's similar to what we usually call intuition, as when we say, "I just know it, but I can't explain how," and the knowing is as incontrovertible as the proverbial nose on your face.

CHAPTER 6

Awakened Awareness in Everyday Life

If you're mindful, you're already creating a separation. Don't be mindful, please! When you walk, just walk. Let the walking walk. Let the talking talk. Let the eating eat, the sitting sit, the working work.

—Zen Master Muho Noelke

Letting go of your identification with the dream character and returning to your true home as the unconditional openness of awakened awareness have a powerful impact on your life at every level. Suddenly the burden of a lifetime has fallen from your shoulders, the dense filters of conditioning have dropped from your eyes, and you experience life with a new freshness, vividness, and clarity. Each moment has intrinsic meaning and value because it shines with the light of awakened awareness, and a subtle, quiet joy becomes your constant companion. Indeed, you realize that happiness is not something you need to earn or that comes and goes capriciously, according to circumstance—it's your natural state, which the conditioning of a lifetime has heretofore hidden from view.

UNCONDITIONAL WELCOMING OF LIFE AS IT UNFOLDS

Because the boundaries between inside and outside have dissolved in the light of awakened awareness, you now recognize that everything you encounter is an expression of what you fundamentally are, your essential true nature and the source of everything. As a result, you meet each situation with an intimacy and a newly discovered confidence and trust that everything is unfolding as it was meant to, informed by a mysterious order that your mind can't comprehend. Because you no longer need "outside" conditions and people to make you happy, you're free to enjoy life just as it is, without having to impose your agenda upon it. Relinquishing your ongoing argument with reality—your struggle, however subtle and insidious, to manipulate it to live up to your expectations—you find yourself welcoming what arises as you would a close friend, never knowing who may appear but remaining open, curious, and unafraid of what the next moment may bring.

Aligned with the natural flow of people and situations, you move through life with ease and a minimum of effort, instead of constantly forcing yourself against the current in order to get your way. Rather than experiencing life through the narrow, me-centered perspective of the separate self, you view it from the expansive, global perspective of awakened awareness and respond appropriately based not on your own personal wants and needs but on the demands of the situation as a whole. Ultimately, the sense of being a separate doer or chooser drops away, because you realize that life is living itself through you, and this bodily being is just a vehicle or vessel for the deeper, all-encompassing wisdom of awakened awareness. Despite the illusion of control, you've never been in charge of your life anyway, never been steering the ship, and now you can trust in the greater movement of life.

In the past, for example, you may have failed to enjoy the fullness and richness of your life, with all its ups and downs, challenges and gifts, because you were so preoccupied with what was lacking and what you could do to make it better. How can I get people to love me? How can I make myself physically comfortable? How can I be a better person? How can I profit from the situation, stand out, gain attention, get ahead? Nor could you appreciate the people closest to you because you kept finding fault and expecting them to change. Now, with the dawning of awakened awareness, you're open to embracing others as they are and receiving what the moment brings, without judgment or manipulation, as you appreciate its perfect imperfection, the radiant indivisible beingness of what presents itself right now. In this open, unconditional, listening presence, everything and everyone unfolds naturally and gracefully without need for constant doing, tweaking, or improving.

Of course, problems continue to arise as before, but rather than being seen as problematic, they're taken as opportunities to stay home and rest in awakened awareness, rather than wandering off into the impenetrable jungle of judgments and reactivity. For example, someone cuts you off in traffic, and the old impulse might be to flip them the finger and let loose with a string of expletives. Instead, you feel the wave of feeling rising and rest back into your own innate happiness and openness and let the feeling move through as you embrace the situation without reacting. Perhaps you're able to recognize that you might have acted exactly as they did, and their inconsiderateness is just a reflection of your own, since we all share the same human impulses and foibles. The old tendencies and reactions may arise briefly but then dissolve in the penetrating light of awakened awareness as you see them for what they are, without indulging or rejecting them.

MEDITATION: Dying into the nondual

Combining elements from several other meditations, this one guides you into a full realization of the boundless, nondual nature of reality, the inseparability of self and other, subject and object, experiencer and experience.

Shift your attention from your thoughts to your bodily sensations. Be aware of the sensations of your body against the chair, your feet against the floor, your hands against your thighs. Be aware of the sensations of your arms and legs, your chest and belly, your neck and head. Be aware of the play of sensations, how they're constantly shifting and changing, and how your awareness dances from sensation to sensation.

If you look closely, you may come to realize that all you can really know of your body are the sensations you're experiencing right now. Everything else is your projection, the image your mind uses to fill in the gaps. For example, you don't experience your whole arm, you just have certain sensations in the vicinity of where you presume your arm to be, and you project the image of an arm upon it.

It's like an impressionist painting. There are thousands of points of color onto which we project a water lily, or a woman, or a building. In the same way, you project the concept "leg" or "head" onto a collection of sensations. Let go of these projections, these concepts, and just be with the sensations as they are, without interpretation.

Notice that surrounding these sensations is open space where no sensation exists at all. In fact, there's far more space than there is sensation, and the sensations are playing or dancing in this space. As you notice the play of sensations in the limitless openness of space, you may become aware that you can't really find a clear dividing line between inside and outside the body; there's just the unbroken field of sensations in space. Notice that thoughts and feelings are playing in the same space, just like sensations.

Now shift the emphasis from the sensations to the space itself. Rest as the awake, aware space in which thoughts, feelings, and sensations arise and pass away. Be the open, unfurnished, limitless, ungraspable space.

Resting as the space, examine the experiences that play in the space. Aside from these experiences, is there anything more you can know directly about the outside world that isn't just a thought or a concept? Doesn't the outside world exist merely as your experience right now? Everything else is a projection, a story.

As you examine your experience, can you find any distinction or difference between the aware space and what arises in the space? Since the world exists only as your experience right now, is there any solid substance out there that's different from the awareness or space in which it's arising? Or are awareness and experience made of the same insubstantial essence?

Sense the inseparability of awareness and the experiences arising in awareness. Inside and outside one indivisible essence. The looker and what's being looked at, one and the same. Rest as the undivided, nondual space of awakened awareness.

UNCONDITIONAL LOVE FOR SELF AND OTHERS

Needless to say, relationships with self and others are transformed in the light of awakened awareness, as you realize that you and the people you encounter are expressions of one undivided reality, the source and essence of all. When you recognize this essential inseparability, the inherent oneness of self and other, not just as a concept but as a direct apperception, an immediate experience, unconditional love naturally arises in your heart not only for others, but for yourself as well. In fact, you recognize that love, like happiness, is your natural state that only a lifetime of conditioning has hidden from view and enclosed and walled away in the heart.

From the perspective of mindfulness as it's generally taught, caring feelings like loving-kindness and compassion must be deliberately and painstakingly cultivated through specific meditation practices—which certainly can have a powerful beneficial effect in enabling you to access the dimension of love. But from the perspective of the direct approach, the realization of your inherent inseparability directly releases and reveals the unconditional love and compassion that already characterize your natural state of open, listening presence. Nothing needs to be developed or cultivated. Just by returning home again and again to awakened awareness, you're bathed in a flow of loving-kindness, appreciation, gratitude, joy, and the other subtle qualities of an open, awakened heart.

No doubt you've had glimpses of this spontaneous arising of unconditional love when you've "fallen in love"—that is, fallen into the love that's always present and available to you. But, like most people, you probably ascribed this powerful feeling to the allure of a significant other and failed to recognize its true nature.

When you're in love, you see the beloved not through the lens of conditioned judgments and personal history, but with fresh eyes that see beyond the imperfections to the essential nature that lies at the core. Awakened awareness gazes upon itself through the eyes of the other and falls in love with itself. Generally, this unconditional love fades as the relationship accumulates a history, you begin to focus on one another's apparent imperfections, and old conditioning kicks into gear once again.

When you recognize and abide in awakened awareness, you see everything and everyone with fresh and open eyes and, as God did in Genesis, find it good, and complete, and inherently lovable. One particular person may elicit in you especially strong feelings of love and attraction, but you know that this person is not the cause of your love and therefore not responsible for how you feel. Rather, you know that love is what you are (and what everything is), and your relationship gives you the possibility of sharing and enjoying this love with another. Paradoxically, you and your beloved are both one and two, separate and inseparable, and relationship offers you the opportunity to dance with this paradox. If you weren't separate, there would be no relationship, no back and forth, no exchange and interaction, no dance. But if you were only separate, there would be no love, or at least the love would be conditional and characterized by constant conflict and negotiation. The beauty of awakened relationship lies in appreciating and cherishing your otherness in light of your oneness, your twoness in light of your inseparability. By maintaining fresh and open eyes and not falling into old patterns, you can keep the relationship perpetually new, alive, and deeply fulfilling. The secret doesn't belong to the other person—it lies in abiding in awakened awareness.

Differences—of preference, predilection, point of view—inevitably arise, but they're not necessarily divisive, because awakened awareness embraces life exactly as it is and has no fixed opinion for or against anything. You like vanilla, and I like chocolate? But of course! You prefer to spend the weekend at home relaxing, but I'd like to take a trip to the country? Naturally, no problem, no reason to argue. Let's listen to one another with open awareness and stay attuned to the flow of the interaction and the resolution that presents itself, rather than attaching ourselves to fixed positions and getting bogged down in conflict. As the French say, *vive la différence!*

Of course, old conditioning inevitably gets triggered, especially in romantic relationships or close friendships, affording you an opportunity to welcome this too just as it is, without judgment or rejection. In fact, once awakened awareness has dawned, intimate relationships offer a uniquely powerful mirror that reveals your stuck places, the areas of your heart and mind where you're still identified with a separate territory and agenda. Rather than hunkering down and defending your position when conflict occurs, your commitment to truth at every level prompts you to investigate in order to discover where you're holding on. Whenever you find yourself reacting with any of the basic conflictual emotions, like anger, fear, hurt, jealousy, or impatience, you have an opportunity to stop and reflect on where you're creating separation, welcome the feelings without acting them out, and investigate the deeper beliefs that perpetuate them. As you ground yourself in the understanding that the problem doesn't lie outside you, but rather arises from the limitations of your own me-centered perspective, you recognize your partner, friend, or family member not as an adversary, but as a ruthless and compassionate teacher in the ongoing process of returning home and abiding in unconditional, nonjudgmental presence. Relationships become profoundly humbling in the best sense because they strip away every identity or position you're attached to and leave you with nothing—except the rawness and richness of this precious moment just as it is.

MEDITATION: Gazing into the eyes of awakened awareness

The very same awareness looks out through every pair of eyes.

Invite a partner or close friend to participate in this meditation with you. Sit face to face, upright yet relaxed, with your knees almost touching. Spend a few minutes with eyes closed as you shift your awareness from your thoughts and feelings to your bodily sensations: the contact of your back and bottom against the seat, your feet against the floor, your hands in your lap, the coming and going of your breath.

Now open your eyes and gaze softly into one another's eyes. The point is not to stare or concentrate, but to extend a relaxed, heartfelt, loving gaze to the eyes of your loved one. If your attention fixates on a particular point or you have difficulty staying present, gently come back to gazing softly into the eyes of the other.

As you continue to gaze, notice what happens. Do you feel uncomfortable, tense, anxious, or ashamed? Do you have judgments or interpretations about yourself or the other person: *I'm not doing it right, he seems angry to me,* or *I don't get the point of this exercise?*

Do you notice any emotions, like flashes of anger, sadness, or regret or waves of joy, gratitude, or love? What happens to the boundaries between you and the other person? Do they become more rigid, or do they begin to blur and dissolve? Continue to gaze in this way for five minutes or longer, welcoming whatever arises without judgment or resistance.

Now consider that the awareness that's looking out through the eyes of the other is the same awareness that's looking out through your eyes. Awareness is gazing upon itself in the form of another. If you feel ready, allow any remaining traces of separation to dissolve in the light of awakened awareness. Inside and outside, self and other, are one undivided field of awareness. Notice any feelings that arise in the heart as you continue to rest in the nondual field for as long as you like.

When you're done, take some time to share your experiences and insights with the other person, as much as you feel comfortable.

EMBRACING YOUR PERFECT IMPERFECTION

As you can see, living from unconditional openness and presence is not about pretending to be some perfect spiritual being surrounded by an aura of love and light—it's about welcoming all of who you are, with all your human baggage and imperfections. Any attempt to live up to some standard of spiritual perfection just mires you in a mind filled with comparisons and self-judgments and sets you at odds with yourself. When you let go of trying to be perfect according to some predetermined idea and let yourself be just as you are, warts and all, your inherent perfection naturally reveals itself, just as the perfection of a tree or a bird reveals itself to your open, nonjudgmental regard. This perfection has nothing to do with the dualistic polarities of perfect and imperfect, good or bad, but refers instead to your precious uniqueness—the fact that no being expresses the same incomparable mix of qualities as you do.

As you rest in this unconditional openness, you no longer feel the need to project an image or defend a position or point of view, and the artificial boundaries between self and others blur and dissolve. As a result, you become more sensitively attuned to the moments when you're acting out of alignment with the truth of your being, not because you're trying to live up to some spiritual ideal but because you can feel the defensiveness and separation arising once again. Out of this natural attunement emerges appropriate action, based not on preestablished precepts of right and wrong, spiritual or nonspiritual, but on the global, all-inclusive view of awakened awareness.

In the eyes of awakened awareness, as I mentioned in chapter 3, "every person and thing, no matter how seemingly flawed or problematic, is perfect in the sense that it simply is as it is, it couldn't possibly be otherwise, and it radiates the essential perfection of Being itself. As a natural response to this recognition there arises a subtle mix of love, wonder, gratitude, and joy." But you may find it far easier to recognize the inherent perfection of plants and animals, sun and sky, loved ones and friends, than to acknowledge and appreciate your own. Indeed, your relationship with yourself may prove to be the most challenging relationship of all—and also the most important. The key is to avoid getting caught in self-judgment and instead welcome your experience just as it is. (For more on relating with emotions and fixated patterns of thinking and reacting, see chapter 7.)

MEDITATION: Welcoming your experience without judgment

Instead of subtly rejecting or attaching to every experience, as you do most of the time, you can practice welcoming it just as it is—another opportunity to rest in the all-inclusive embrace of awakened awareness.

For the next two hours (or longer, if you like), say yes to whatever you're experiencing. Say yes to the difficult feelings, the negative thoughts, the challenging tasks, the people, the weather, the news, the sounds, the smells. By yes, I mean not resignation or defeat, but heartfelt acknowledgment.

In the process, you may notice the many ways your mind keeps saying *no* to life—suppressing your feelings and thoughts, judging other people, refusing to accept the way things are. You may be amazed to discover how much energy your mind consumes by refusing to accept what's actually happening right in front of you.

Instead, for the next two hours or longer, notice your tendency to resist or deny and instead say yes: yes to your hunger and longing, yes to your anger and fear, yes to your partner or kids, yes to your body and face, yes to your life. As much as possible, rest in the unconditional openness of awakened awareness. Of course, you're welcome to say no as necessary or change what you don't like, but take a moment to say yes first.

You may be so accustomed to saying no that you don't know how to say yes at first. So feel free to repeat the word "yes" to yourself to help get you started. Maybe you'll end up enjoying the dance of yes so much that you extend it to every area of your life. Yes, yes, yes!

DYING BEFORE YOU DIE

When you discover that you're not the contents of your life—the body, mind, thoughts, feelings, family, friends, accomplishments, relationships, and material possessions you took yourself to be—but the boundariless space or context in which your life unfolds, you die to an old, time-bound identity and discover yourself as the eternal. Recognizing that who you really are is the ground of being—the ungraspable, immaterial, indestructible essence that remains, unchanging, when everything else is stripped away—you discover a confidence and a courage in the deathless that pain, disease, old age, and death can't shake. As the old Zen masters say, "Die before you die, and mortality can't disturb you anymore."

At the same time, you may still have strong preferences for being healthy, vital, and free of pain, and you may feel disappointed, frightened, frustrated, or grief-stricken at the onset of serious illness or infirmity. Sickness, old age, and death are among the most intense and relentless of human experiences. Yet beneath the waves of natural human feeling lie the deep peace and surrender of awakened awareness, as well as a deeply rooted trust in the sacred mystery of life. "Not my will but Thy will be done" is not merely a prayer of complete obeisance, it's a description of the way things actually are. After all, you've never been in charge, even for an instant, and surrender is just an acknowledgment of what has always been the case.

CREATING A SUPPORTIVE ENVIRONMENT FOR AWAKENED AWARENESS TO THRIVE

The more steadily you abide in awakened awareness, and the more consistently you come home once your attention has strayed, the better able you are to meet even the most challenging life circumstances with grace and ease. In the beginning, however, as you're still learning to live from this radically different perspective, you may find it helpful to simplify your life as much as you can and afford yourself ample time for quiet reflection and self-inquiry. As one of my teachers used to say, work as much as you need to, and spend the rest of your time living in beauty. Otherwise, the complexity of life's demands may become so pressing that you're left with precious little time for just being.

Here are a few things you can do to allow more time and space in your life for living from awakened awareness:

- Spend time each day sitting quietly, being present, inquiring.

- Savor the beauty that each moment affords.

- Enjoy your time with loved ones and friends, rather than playing with your smartphone or tablet.

- Make time on the weekends for being in nature without digital devices of any kind.

- Maintain separate phones and e-mail addresses for work and personal matters.

- Don't take your work home with you, and avoid checking work e-mails after hours.

- Turn off your phone at least an hour before bed.

- Rather than consulting your e-mail or social networks yet again, be still and rest in the moment.

Of course, you can't get your life to be exactly as you'd like it—in fact, you have precious little control over how circumstances unfold. But you can allow the emphasis of your life to shift from the conventional goals of accomplishment and self-improvement to the subtler and more insubstantial purpose of aligning yourself with the deepest truth of your being. You can't put a price tag on this approach or easily explain it to colleagues and family members who may think you should put more emphasis on working harder and getting ahead. But once you've tasted the peace and joy of your natural state of openness and presence, you'll find yourself drawn inexorably back again and again—and your priorities and preoccupations will shift in response.

IN CLOSING

As you rest and abide as awakened awareness, your life transforms at every level. Instead of striving to change or improve it, you welcome it as it is and find joy in its inherent mystery, beauty, and perfection. Relationships that had been marked by conflict and dissatisfaction, including the relationship with yourself, are now filled with mutual appreciation, gratitude, and love. In fact, in the absence of an agenda, an ongoing argument with reality, you naturally fall in love with what is.

I don't understand how you can face death with equanimity without a belief in an afterlife of some kind.

If you take yourself to be a collection of thoughts, feelings, memories, stories, accomplishments, and beliefs, you can't peacefully accept the death of the physical body, unless you believe that the separate self that the body apparently contains gets reincarnated or reborn in some way, whether into heaven, paradise, or some future human form. In order to ease the fear of death, many religions, including Buddhism, offer a comforting explanation for what happens after death. But when you wake up out of the dream of being a separate someone bound by the body–mind and recognize your identity with the limitless, formless, all-pervasive essence of what is (which I have been calling awakened awareness), death loses its sting because you realize with every fiber of your being that who you really are can never die. What a liberating revelation!

I know myself too well to believe I'm inherently perfect. If I don't make a constant effort to improve myself, I'm sure I'll just keep repeating the same self-destructive behaviors again and again.

The problem with self-improvement is that your constant effort to live up to some idea of how your life should be can be exhausting and generally has only limited effectiveness. Besides, you might want to take a look at where you got your idea. Did you formulate it based on what you read in a popular magazine or self-help bestseller or saw on *Oprah* or *Dr. Phil?* Did you glean it from teachings about how a spiritual person should look? Or is it the product of childhood conditioning, rooted in what your parents and their parents believed? You can spend a lifetime in endless dissatisfaction trying to be someone you're not, comparing yourself with standards that may shift and change with the winds of popular culture or your own interests and life experience. Or you can find happiness and contentment right now by embracing yourself just as you are, which is what the great sages recommend.

The fact is, the separate self you're struggling to improve inevitably feels inadequate because it has no abiding substance or validity. At best, it's a flimsy shadow of who you really are, a pale imposter posing as the truth at the core of your being. No matter how much you improve it, you'll never be satisfied with it because it can't provide the unconditional happiness and peace you seek. Instead, stop trying to be perfect and let yourself be as you are. Paradoxically, this deep self-acceptance and letting be is the most powerful self-improvement because it puts an end to your divisive, conflictual relationship with yourself. From this place of deep letting go and letting be, happiness reveals itself to be your natural state, and action spontaneously arises that's appropriate to the circumstances at hand.

CHAPTER 7

Your Head in the Demon's Mouth

From the perspective of awakened awareness, emotions are not problems to solve, but experiences to welcome, without indulging them or acting them out.

Perhaps nothing in human experience is more mysterious and confounding than the powerful pull of turbulent emotions like rage, grief, terror, jealousy, or lust. They seem to operate according to their own laws and retain only a tenuous connection with the so-called rational mind, which has long struggled to make sense of them. Indeed, they can appear to exist in a nether realm all their own. They cloud our judgment, incite us to act in strange and self-destructive ways, and appear to prevent us from abiding in the peace and clarity of awakened awareness.

Buddha dubbed craving (originally, *tanha*, "thirst") the root cause of suffering and taught a path to free ourselves from it. The hermits, renunciates, yogis, and *sadhus* of every religious tradition have spent lifetimes trying to find peace from powerful emotions by eliminating or transcending them. More recently, Freud and his successors in the field of Western psychology have endeavored to discover what causes them and how we can release the stranglehold they have on us. And pharmaceutical companies have developed medications that promise to mute or suppress them.

From the perspective of our natural state of unconditional openness and presence, however, emotions are not problems to solve; they're just experiences to be welcomed as they are, without indulging them or acting them out.

RELATING TO EMOTIONS FROM A CONVENTIONAL PERSPECTIVE

If you're like most people, you've been conditioned to relate to difficult emotions in a number of ways. Perhaps the most common is to identify with them and become immersed in the story that perpetuates them. For example, if your lover rejects you for another, you may indulge in stories about what a horrible person he is while wallowing in feelings of anger, bitterness, and despair. Or if you lose your job, you may blame your boss and run her down to your friends while being staunchly unwilling to face your own unskillful behavior. You're awash in painful emotions and lost in the endless drama that plays out in your mind.

Another common response is to avoid the feelings by employing one or more of the so-called defense mechanisms like suppression, repression, projection, sublimation, or projective identification. Generally unconscious and therefore difficult to spot, these complex psychological processes prevent you from facing and embracing the challenging emotions by hiding them or attributing them to others. For example, you don't need to deal with your own pain and vulnerability because the other people in your life appear like helpless victims to you. Or you succeed in maintaining your well-honed persona as the good guy who never gets ruffled by burying your anger deep inside. The problem with this approach is that the misplaced and misunderstood emotions may cause illness, tension, conflict with others, and a feeling of being cut off from your own vitality and authenticity.

Finally, you may attempt to transcend your feelings (a kind of defense mechanism popular in spiritual circles) by hiding out in detachment and disengagement, pretending you're too evolved to have "negative" emotions. If you're involved in an intimate relationship, your partner may keep calling you out on your holier-than-thou attitude, which tends to preclude the possibility of genuine intimacy, until the facade crumbles. Or you may spend your life in a kind of isolated limbo as the so-called negative emotions continue to express themselves in unconscious ways. Known as spiritual bypassing, this approach has proved to be common among spiritual teachers in the West, who may profess infallibility while raging at their underlings, having sex with their students, and embezzling ashram funds.

RELATING TO EMOTIONS WITH MINDFULNESS AND AWAKENED AWARENESS

If you practice mindfulness meditation, you may take a very different approach. Instead of defending against your feelings or acting them out, you may learn to make friends with them by offering them your gentle, nonjudgmental attention. Over time you may develop an inner spaciousness that allows you to be aware of thoughts and feelings without necessarily getting caught up in them. When strong emotions do grip you, you can explore them with compassionate awareness and gain insight into their makeup and the circumstances that may be triggering them.

With careful investigation, you may discover that emotions are composed of thoughts, memories, images, and bodily sensations, and you may be able to gain insight into their ephemeral, insubstantial nature, which eventually frees you from their grasp. In Buddhism and other traditions, mindfulness is often accompanied by meditations for cultivating more positive, life-affirming emotions like loving-kindness, compassion, joy, and equanimity as antidotes for more destructive emotions like anger, hatred, jealousy, and fear. Ultimately, with more advanced practice, you may be able to penetrate the insubstantiality of the separate self you take yourself to be—and in whom these difficult emotions apparently occur. (For a more detailed discussion of mindfulness of emotions, see my book *Meditation for Dummies*.)

In practice, however, mindfulness meditation may tend to perpetuate a detached, aloof, witnessing position that subtly pushes away certain feelings as too intense or threatening and encourages the use of awareness to control your mental and emotional state. Rather than allowing your carefully orchestrated calm to be shattered by difficult emotions like anger or grief, you may use mindfulness to bypass or suppress them and enforce a peace of mind that's dependent on sustaining your mindfulness through constant effort. As soon as you feel your equanimity crumbling, you rush back to your seat for another dose of meditation.

By contrast, awakened awareness spontaneously welcomes and embraces emotions just as they are, without any deliberate effort to investigate, manage, suppress, or change them in any way. The emphasis shifts from the emotions themselves to the unconditional openness in which the emotions arise and pass away. Resting as this openness, this pure and timeless presence, and knowing it to be your fundamental true nature, you have no argument with any experience and allow it to be just as it is. You don't preference so-called positive emotions as more desirable than so-called negative or destructive ones, yet paradoxically this unconditional welcoming naturally gives rise to a fullness of heart and nourishing feelings of peace, love, gratitude, and joy.

Indeed, without any effort or deliberate cultivation or intention on your part, these nourishing and replenishing emotions gradually penetrate and dissipate the core patterns and stuck places that may continue to give rise to conflictual emotions and to cloud awakened awareness. The more you rest in and as awakened awareness, the more you undermine the obstacles to living it more fully and continuously—and the more you release their energy to empower a more awakened life.

MEDITATION: Connecting with unconditional openness and purity

Adapted from the Tibetan tradition, this meditation uses visualization as a doorway to resting in your natural state.

Take a few minutes to sit comfortably, with your eyes closed, as you shift your attention from your thinking mind to the coming and going of your breath. Now imagine, perched on the crown of your head, a radiant being of infinite purity, light, and love. Perhaps it takes the form of Jesus, the Buddha, Mother Mary, Kwan Yin, or a particular angel, bodhisattva, deity, saint, or sage. Or you may just imagine a luminous sphere. Whatever form it takes, don't focus on the details but on the light and love that it radiates. Imagine this being with all your senses.

Imagine that this light and love radiate out in every direction, extending farther and farther until they reach the farthest corners of the universe. Imagine the whole universe filled with the energy of light and love, peace and joy. Spend a few minutes enjoying this imagery.

Now imagine this energy flowing like a river of white light down through your head and neck, filling your body with love and light. Imagine that this pure, expansive energy dissolves all contraction and fixation and leaves you feeling cleansed and purified.

Now imagine this being of light descending through your spine and coming to rest in your heart, where you merge with it and become it. You are a being of infinite purity, light, and love, radiating these qualities out from the heart in every direction. Continue to rest as this infinite radiance for as long you feel inclined.

Finally, let go of all imagery and just rest in your natural state of intrinsic purity, peace, love, and joy. Notice how this meditation continues to affect you as you get up and go about your day.

If you feel moved to explore your emotions, you can remove any labels, concepts, or stories and invite the direct, unmediated experience of the emotion itself. When you stop resisting it, trying to get rid of it, or even making an effort to be mindful of it, but just let it be as it is in open, unconditional awareness, you may discover that it's merely a movement of energy, one of the many movements in the dance we call living. Only because you perpetuate it with a story or struggle to tame or antidote it does it pose a problem. Left to its own natural unfolding, it eventually releases in a process some traditions call self-liberation. Over time, you learn to recognize that these emotions don't belong to you—or more precisely, there's no permanent and abiding you to whom these emotions belong—and they naturally pass through with nowhere to stick.

Although awakened awareness does not harbor a preference for positive or negative emotions, it does, by its very nature, prefer freedom and openness to fixation and contraction. Even the attachment to positive feelings and mind-states can interfere with the full embrace of experience just as it is, which is the mark of nondual awareness. As soon as you get caught in picking and choosing, you're once again thrust into the realm of duality, of preferring positive over negative, good over bad, right over wrong, light over dark, and you're resisting the reality that presents itself now.

The difference between mindfulness and the direct approach is subtle but significant: Mindfulness employs a special state of penetrating attention to gain insight into challenging emotions for the purpose of releasing them and replacing them with their more easeful alternatives. The direct approach naturally and spontaneously welcomes emotions without any agenda or plan—and without any identification with them as belonging to me—and trusts that they will self-liberate in the unconditional space of awakened awareness.

MEDITATION: Welcoming emotions just as they are

Strong emotions may seem like hindrances or distractions that prevent you from resting in awareness. But if you welcome them as they are without getting caught up in the content, they too can point you back to your inherent wakefulness and peace.

Take a few minutes to sit comfortably and shift your attention from your thinking mind to the coming and going of your breath. Now check in with your body to see if you can find a lingering feeling of anger, sadness, or fear. If you can't sense anything specific, you can bring to mind a difficult recent event and notice the feelings it evokes.

Choose one of the feelings and let your awareness rest there, not with the story but with the sensations in the body. Let go of any images, memories, or thoughts that may arise and just be with the sensations, without trying to change or get rid of them. Even let go of labels like "anger," "sadness," or "fear," which have strong connotations, and just be with the raw feeling itself. Notice any resistance you might have to facing the feeling and allow that to be there as well.

Now pay attention to the stories that keep arising around the feeling, not in order to indulge them but merely to become intimate with them. Are these stories familiar? Have you told these same stories before? How do you react when you lean into the story and believe it? What happens when you step back and see it as just a story? Is this story true? What kind of a price do you pay for believing it?

Now return to the bare feeling without overlay. Has it shifted or changed in any way? Whether it's changed or not, let it be as it is as you let go of any effort to be present and just rest as the open expanse of awareness itself. Let the feeling unfold (or not) without any further intervention or effort on your part. Let it be just another piece of driftwood afloat on the limitless ocean of who you are.

IN THE GRASP OF POWERFUL EMOTIONS

From time to time, you may be gripped by powerful emotions and feel like you've lost your connection with the ground of awakened awareness as you're swept along by the torrent. Rather than struggling to stay present and mindful, one approach is to just let yourself be taken, as you would if you were being tossed around by waves in the ocean, without deliberately indulging them or acting them out. Let them run their course without resistance. Then, when the torrent subsides, you can lift your head above water and assess the situation. Perhaps you can reflect on where you got hooked in and identified, the core stories or beliefs that seduced you back into separation and conflict.

For example, your boss gives you some critical feedback during your annual review at work, and you immediately drop into feelings of panic and dread, as you imagine that your job is at risk and your survival at stake. No matter how much you try to reason with yourself, the emotions feel like they're going to overwhelm you. If you practice mindfulness, you may find it helpful to keep returning to your breath as an anchor as you struggle to gain some perspective on these powerful feelings. Or, as before, you can remove any labels, concepts, or stories and invite the direct, unmediated experience of the emotions themselves, allowing them to run their course with the confidence that this unconditional allowing itself is your homeground of awakened awareness. Then, when the emotions subside, you can inquire into the core beliefs that gave rise to them in the first place, such as "I don't have what it takes to survive," or "I'm not safe in the world." As the beliefs lose their hold in light of a deeper knowing, you can spontaneously return to abide in the nondual field of awakened awareness.

The main point here is that you're not struggling to change the experience in any way, not even by efforting to be mindful. You're letting the emotions be as they are and move as they do, knowing that they can't destroy who you really are. In fact, the more you resist, the more you reinforce the sense of separation on which the emotions are based. Paradoxically, the more you embrace them, the more they loosen their grip. One great meditation master reported that when he resisted the demons that inhabited his cave, they just became fiercer. But when he welcomed them to share the cave with him—finally putting his head into the mouth of the fiercest of all—they disappeared and never returned.

No matter how many times you get carried away, resist the temptation to judge certain experiences as bad and to beat yourself up for having them. Judgment just adds more stress and conflict to the mix and ends up intensifying the emotions rather than softening them. Recognize that emotions come and go like the weather and can't be controlled—but resting in awareness changes your relationship to them. As much as possible, be the warm and welcoming space in which the emotions play themselves out, but don't get drawn into the fray—and when you do, notice your reactivity and come back home again.

WHAT DO EMOTIONS MEAN?

The Buddhist tradition recognizes two different ways of relating to life: the absolute and relative perspectives. From the absolute perspective, everything is perfect and complete just as it is, yet at the same time empty of abiding substance, like a dream that seems meaningful but is ultimately evanescent and insubstantial. From this perspective, you're a dream character whose task is to wake up from your slumber and realize your true nature as pure, unconditional awareness, apart from the dream. From the relative perspective, you're an individual person who interacts with other individuals, gets involved in intimate relationships, has personal preferences and a sense of purpose, makes a living, assumes responsibilities, and faces the consequences of your actions. You answer to a particular name, wake up in this body and not another, put food in this mouth, live in this house, have these friends and family. Both perspectives are true simultaneously; indeed, they're inseparable, like flip sides of the same coin or like a box and its lid, as one teaching puts it. If you get stuck in the relative and forget the absolute, you only identify with your appearance in form and suffer the slings and arrows of outrageous fortune without a deeper understanding of the ground of being to sustain you. If you get stuck in the absolute and neglect the relative, you end up feeling detached and aloof from life and other people, and you don't give rise to the love and compassion that mark the expression of awakened awareness in the realm of form.

From an absolute perspective, emotions don't belong to anyone; they're just a movement of energy in the dream and don't have personal meaning because there's no abiding person to whom they belong. But at a relative level, some emotions do have meaning because they signify stirrings in the heart that have currency in the realm of friendship, family, and intimate relationship. For example, some people naturally evoke certain feelings in you that can't be denied and that become the basis for how you act in the world. In fact, a sensitive attunement to the play of feelings, felt senses, and intuitions forms the basis for healthy, awakened relationships and gives direction and purpose to life. The key is to discern the difference between reactive emotions and essential human emotions—what one of my teachers called emotionality and true emotion.

Emotionality is based on conditioning, the stories and beliefs that fuel your identification with a limited, me-centered point of view. Someone challenges your carefully crafted self-image, for example, and you lash out with anger or hurt and create conflict and separation. Reactive emotions tend to be intense, painful, disruptive, targeted at others, and defensive, as if you're trying to protect an inner fortress or vulnerable place that feels like it's besieged. Though they may fade with time, they tend to accumulate and won't release and self-liberate unless you gently inquire into the core beliefs that perpetuate the sense of separation on which they're based.

By contrast, essential emotions and felt senses are subtler, quieter, not as distinct or hard-edged, and not based on stories and beliefs about how the world and other people should be. Rather than being painful and conflictual, they tend to foster relatedness and intimacy, not only with others, but with yourself as well. When you welcome true emotions and experience them fully, you often feel relieved, energized, tender, touched, and more intimate with your own being.

For example, if a friend dies, you may feel a grief and loss that open you to a greater appreciation of the other person and a profound gratitude for life itself. Or, if you have a misunderstanding with a loved one, your hurt may naturally resolve into compassion and understanding for everyone concerned. Because these emotions and felt senses tend to arise directly from the heart, rather than from areas of conflict and tension, they often reveal an inner knowing that informs and enriches your life in form. (For a thorough exploration of attuning to feelings and felt senses, I recommend the book *In Touch* by John Prendergast.)

RELATING WITH FIXATED PATTERNS OF THINKING AND FEELING

As you allow emotions to play out in awareness without interfering with or manipulating them in any way, you may begin to notice that they keep circling back to the same repetitive patterns of thinking and feeling as the mind habitually fixates on certain issues and concerns. Indeed, the tendency for the mind to fixate in some way is the root cause of suffering, out of which the reactive emotions arise. Once you become familiar with these repetitive patterns, the recurrent stories that keep hooking you back into identification and struggle, you can recognize them more quickly when they get activated and more readily let go of the emotions they generate and invite them to pass through.

Let's say, for example, that your core story is "Nobody loves me"—and even more fundamentally, "I'm unlovable." You filter your relationships through the lens of this story and find evidence for it everywhere. Your best friend doesn't call you for a week, and you assume she doesn't care about you. Your colleagues at work forget to invite you to lunch, and you conclude they can't stand to be around you. You walk around with a constant feeling of hurt and rejection that colors your relationships at every level—and that may even make you less lovable to others. But once you see through this pattern and recognize it as the distortion you impose upon reality, rather than what other people are actually doing to you, you can catch it when it arises yet again and nip those familiar feelings of rejection and hurt in the bud, before they proliferate.

In fact, one of the most effective ways to return to awakened awareness is to become intimately familiar with your core stories and meet them with compassion and insight as they arise. You don't have to make an effort to do this deliberately; once recognized, your natural state of unconditional openness spontaneously moves back toward painful stories and emotions in an (effortless) attempt to liberate and reclaim them by infusing them with awareness. Like water, which flows into every available nook and crevice, the light of awakened awareness seems to have an innate tendency to penetrate the dark and unconscious areas of our lives.

Beyond individual core stories, each person has a habitual pattern of fixating on particular recurring themes that runs like a unifying thread through his or her life. Over the centuries, these fixations have been articulated in different ways in different cultures and traditions. For example, Buddhism categorizes these patterns into three primary types: greed, aversion, and delusion, based on the three traditional "poisons" or causes of suffering. Greed types focus on what they want and can't get enough of— food, sex, attention, pleasure, relationships, material possessions. As a result, their emotions gravitate toward permutations of desire, like lust, hunger, avarice, hurt, or jealousy. Aversion types, as their name implies, focus on fending off perceived threats or attacks from outside, generally through some version of anger or fear, for example, anxiety, dread, criticism, hypervigilance, hatred, or rage. And delusion types generally live in a haze of confusion, ignorance, and disorganization, with emotions that tend to be more muted, mixed, ambivalent, and unclear.

The Sufi tradition developed an even more sophisticated way of understanding the core ways we fixate our attention and interpret life based on our fixation (which was then further elaborated in the West) known as the Enneagram, a nine-faceted system based on three fundamental types: image, fear, and anger. The three image types are concerned with how they're perceived and received by others; they relate primarily through the heart and are preoccupied with helping others, appearing competent and successful, or establishing themselves as uniquely creative. The three fear types are concerned with figuring things out through the mind, in order to stay safe in a threatening or uncertain world, create an elaborate and protective inner world, or avoid unpleasant feelings by strategizing to keep life interesting. And the anger types are focused on dealing with their own aggressive impulses by suppressing them, acting them out by dominating others, or channeling them into judgment and one-upmanship. (This synopsis is extremely simplistic and merely intended to give a flavor of the system. For extensive elaborations of each type, I recommend *The Wisdom of the Enneagram* by Don Riso and Russ Hudson and *From Fixation to Freedom* by Eli Jaxon-Bear.)

MEDITATION: Identifying your fixation

Ever wonder about your own core fixation, the habitual way you organize your attention and filter your experience of life? Here's a meditation for reflecting on the key themes and strategies that lie at the heart of your fixation. Remember, your fixation is not who you are, it's what prevents you from fully being who you are.

Take a few minutes to sit comfortably and shift your attention from your thinking mind to the coming and going of your breath. Now bring to mind three or four recent events that triggered painful feelings in you. If you don't tend to feel things strongly, just bring to mind situations where you experienced conflict or stress. Take some time to examine them more closely in retrospect and reflect on the issues that may have triggered your pain.

Do you notice any recurring emotions or themes that run like threads through each situation? What do you tend to believe about life? Are you primarily concerned with getting people to love and approve of you? Or are you trying to protect yourself from attack or criticism in a world you perceive as unsafe? Do you tend to respond to difficulties by trying to figure things out, by reacting from a gut instinctual level, or by connecting with others? What are your core strategies for dealing with life? What are your primary recurring emotions?

Take note of what you discover, and at the same time notice how this recognition affects you. Do you feel more spacious and less reactive now? Or are you still caught up in the story?

Now notice that your answers to these questions, and the questions themselves, are just thoughts and concepts arising in your awareness. Notice any tendency to attach to them or create stories about them. Let them pass through like any other thought that might arise in your awareness. Let yourself rest as awareness itself. Be the space in which these thoughts, emotions, and stories come and go. Remember that you are not the story—the story arises in you.

As helpful as these and other typologies may be for recognizing your own core fixations and explaining the seemingly inexplicable behavior of others, they're misleading if they seduce you into believing that your fixation is a description of who you really are and then using this knowledge to solidify your identification with a separate self. From the perspective of awakened awareness, the Enneagram and other typologies are useful only in articulating and clarifying what you're not, so you can see your fixation for what it is and immediately return to your homeground of unconditional openness and presence. When you get trapped in a core story and can't readily find your way back to openness, you can remind yourself of your fixation and quickly see the current story as an expression of the deeper pattern. Otherwise, it's just a mind game that has no deeper significance and can devolve into another distraction or preoccupation. In other words, you can end up being fixated on fixation.

Ultimately, any fixation, even on exalted spiritual beliefs, insights, or states, can become an obstacle to the complete and unconditional openness and freedom of awakened awareness. Your true nature can't be identified or circumscribed in any way, and the mind's tendency to categorize and conceptualize only obscures it. Any understanding must dissolve in being understanding, that is, you need to let go of your spiritual ideas and concepts and simply abide as the emptiness and freedom you know yourself to be.

IN CLOSING

Did you ever see the movie *The Little Buddha*, in which the meditating soon-to-be enlightened teacher is tempted by an onslaught of powerful images and emotions? He remains tranquil and undisturbed, and enlightenment, like the morning star, finally dawns. Once you discover your natural state of inherent wakefulness and peace, it can feel as if all the conditioning of a lifetime is conspiring to seduce you away. The key to continuing to abide as awakened awareness is to resist the temptation to struggle and resist and instead, like the Buddha, welcome the experiences just as they are. In the process, you can become familiar with the particular patterns of preoccupation and fixation that keep hooking you back in and gradually release their hold over you.

You seem to be suggesting that emotions are inevitably caused by underlying beliefs. But I sometimes have powerful negative feelings that arise for no apparent reason I can detect. Is it possible that some feelings just happen?

Yes, it's certainly possible, especially with emotions that result from early life (or powerful adult-life) trauma. For example, you may find yourself in the most seemingly innocuous situation and suddenly feel terrified and have no idea why. Most likely, you're being triggered by an association between the current circumstances and past events that were harmful, dangerous, or abusive. For example, certain sexual situations may trigger fear in someone who was abused as a child, or the backfiring of a car may terrify a war veteran whose buddies were shot on his watch. If you investigate more closely, you'll often find core beliefs like "I'm not safe" or "The world is out to get me," that were not readily apparent at first. Whether you can identify core beliefs or not, the main point is to welcome the feelings without trying to resist or change them in any way.

I'm rarely disturbed by difficult emotions, and I believe it's because of all the meditation I've done. But my wife just thinks I'm hiding out in detachment and disengagement, as you describe. How can I tell which of us is right?

Here are a few questions you can honestly ask yourself: Am I emotionally available and responsive when the situation calls for it? Or am I withdrawn and unable to feel? For example, my child describes some happy experiences he had at school. Or my wife tells me about some challenging interactions at work. Do I feel myself empathically moved and connected? Or do I watch from a distance, like the Vulcans in *Star Trek*? Abiding in awakened awareness doesn't remove you from the ordinary realm of human feeling; rather, it enables even more intimacy and connectedness without the knee-jerk reactivity that comes from defending a position or point of view.

Are you saying that it's possible to experience awakened awareness and simultaneously have negative, destructive, or angry thoughts and feelings?

Definitely. All thoughts and feelings are welcome in awakened awareness. Remember that awakened awareness is not an experience, but the awake, aware space in which experiences come and go. It doesn't prefer one experience over another and doesn't try to edit or suppress what arises. Indeed, through the eyes of awakened awareness all thoughts and feelings, whether positive or negative, are equally empty and insubstantial, like clouds that shift and change across the sky but have no abiding meaning or essence. The more you rest as awakened awareness and allow thoughts and feelings to pass through without grasping or identifying with them, the more they lose their hold over you.

I can't really see myself in any of the fixations you describe—or more accurately, I see myself in all of them. Is it possible to share a little of every personality type?

Yes, of course, though one type or fixation generally predominates. Needless to say we're all motivated by fear, anger, ignorance, and self-image at times, and we all want people to love and approve of us, try to figure things out in order to protect ourselves, and suppress our feelings to avoid conflict at times. But if you look closely, you'll probably find that one particular strategy tends to recur repeatedly and have pride of place. In the end, though, don't get fixated on fixations—they're merely descriptions of what you're not and have ultimate value only as pointers to what you are.

Deconstructing and Deepening

In your absence is your presence.

—Jean Klein

In the end, your homeground of awakened awareness is a groundless ground; there's no there there, no location, no substance, nothing to grasp or attain, no place to land. By its very nature, unconditional openness is not limited by any conditions; it's pure potential, boundless, unfurnished space without center or edge. Even this space is not separate from what it contains; awareness and the objects of awareness are one and inseparable. There is only this indivisible, nondual reality. Just This!

Although we use a phrase to describe it, awakened awareness is not some separate state or thing. As soon as you think you've found something you can hold onto and name, you've lost your way and become entangled in concepts and experiences. You can never grasp it as you would a thought or emotion or any other object of awareness—you can only be it knowingly and allow it to live you, in a way the mind can't comprehend.

As you read these words, you may find them abstract, or even unintelligible to your rational mind. Yet a deeper place inside already knows the truth of what's being said and resonates with it as a tuning fork resonates with a bell that's struck at the same frequency.

Paradoxically, the only way to deepen awakened awareness is to let go of it completely. You can never deliberately elaborate or improve it because as soon as you try, it eludes your grasp. From an absolute perspective, of course, awakened awareness can't deepen because it's already boundless; what deepens is your ability to rest in it. As my teacher Jean Klein used to say, in your absence is your presence—the more you let go and let be, the deeper is the abiding as awareness without anyone abiding or trying to be aware.

The mark of resting and abiding in awakened awareness is that you no longer feel any lack or insufficiency, no longer feel the need to change, adjust, add to, or subtract from the present moment. You're not looking for some better, more fulfilling, more comfortable state—you're complete and content with everything just as it is. Not that you wouldn't make changes in your environment or situation as a natural movement toward balance and ease—anything from putting on a sweater or going for a walk to buying a new car or changing jobs—it's just that you don't *require* anything to be different, and you're at peace whether things change or not. Though circumstances are constantly shifting and unfolding and you may like or not like what's arising now, there's a deeper knowing that there's always and only This, just as it is. The recognition that This is what you are, fundamentally and essentially, marks the realization of awakened awareness.

As your realization ripens, awakened awareness permeates your life, and all traces of a separate someone drop away. Ultimately, you can't even say, "I am awakened awareness" because there's no I left to identify or not. Only awakened awareness remains—the nondual, indivisible continuum, the One without a second, expressing itself in a myriad of forms. Just This!

Stephan Bodian is a teacher in the non-dual wisdom tradition of Zen and Advaita a pioneer in the integration of Eastern wisdom and Western psychology, and an internationally recognized expert on meditation and mindfulness. His books include *Wake Up Now* and the guidebook *Meditation for Dummies*. A licensed psychotherapist, he leads classes, workshops, and retreats in the direct approach to spiritual realization and offers counseling and mentoring to people worldwide. www.stephanbodian.org

Foreword writer **John J. Prendergast, PhD,** is author of *In Touch*, senior editor of *The Sacred Mirror* and *Listening from the Heart of Silence*, and retired adjunct professor of psychology at the California Institute of Integral Studies in San Francisco. He is a spiritual teacher and also a psychotherapist in private practice. www.listeningfromsilence.com

MORE BOOKS for the SPIRITUAL SEEKER

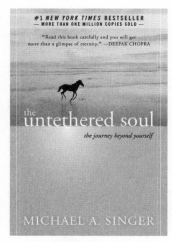
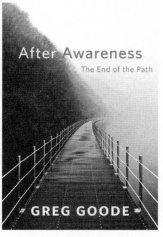
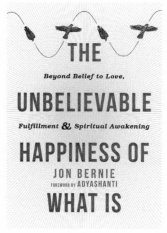

newharbingerpublications

NON-DUALITY PRESS | SAHAJA | REVEAL PRESS